Library of
Davidson College

PSYCHOLOGY
AND SOCIAL CHANGE

Psychology and the Problems of Society

Kenneth J. Gergen, Consulting Editor
Swarthmore College

Ashmore and McConahay:
Psychology and America's Urban Dilemmas

Kidder and Stewart:
The Psychology of Intergroup Relations
Conflict and Consciousness

Pizer and Travers:
Psychology and Social Change

PSYCHOLOGY AND SOCIAL CHANGE

Stuart A. Pizer
Harvard University

Jeffrey R. Travers
Swarthmore College

McGRAW-HILL BOOK COMPANY

New York/St. Louis/San Francisco/Düsseldorf/Johannesburg
Kuala Lumpur/London/Mexico/Montreal/New Delhi/Panama
Paris/São Paulo/Singapore/Sydney/Tokyo/Toronto

301.24
P695p

Psychology and Social Change

Copyright © 1975 by McGraw-Hill, Inc. All rights reserved.
Printed in the United States of America. No part of this publication
may be reproduced, stored in a retrieval system, or transmitted, in any
form or by any means, electronic, mechanical, photocopying, recording, or
otherwise, without the prior written permission of the publisher.

1 2 3 4 5 6 7 8 9 0 B P B P 7 9 8 7 6 5 4

This book was set in Press Roman by Allen Wayne Technical
Corp. The editor was Richard R. Wright;
the cover was designed by J. E. O'Connor;
the cover illustration by Cathy Hull;
the production supervisor was Milton J. Heiberg.
The Book Press, Inc., was printer and binder.

Library of Congress Cataloging in Publication Data

Pizer, Stuart A
  Psychology and social change.

  (Psychology and the problems of society)
  1. Social change. 2. Social groups. 3. Sociali-
zation. I. Travers, Jeffrey R., joint author.
II. Title. [DNLM: 1. Psychology. 2. Psychology,
Social. 3. Social change. HM251 P695p 1975]
HM101.P55   301.24'01'9   74-10063   75-5190
ISBN 0-07-050224-2

Contents

Foreword	vii
Acknowledgments	ix
Chapter 1 Introduction	1
Chapter 2 Psychology and Change in Individuals	9
Chapter 3 Psychology and Change in Groups	33
Chapter 4 Psychology and Change in Institutions	80
Chapter 5 Psychology and Change in Society	123
Epilogue	156
Bibliography	159
Index	169

Foreword

> *Between the idea*
> *And the reality . . .*
> *Falls the Shadow*

T. S. Eliot
The Hollow Men

When properly executed, psychological research narrows the distance between idea and reality. We conceive of a world in which conflict and suffering are not commonplace occurrences, in which immense investments of human energy and resources are not absorbed by institutions holding our numbers under lock and key. We have conceptions of a world in which people truly seem concerned over the wellbeing of others and are willing to sacrifice their interests for the common good. And yet, the void between such ideals and the realities of daily life is such that one can scarcely avoid scepticism. Psychology, like the other socio-behavioral sciences, appears to offer us a means of altering our condition. It holds out promise that, with proper application of its methods, we can penetrate the processes locking us into our present state. Further, we can determine how to break the present patterns and build a more fulfilling future. When properly executed, psychology may enable us to more closely approximate our conceptions of the good society.

The present volume is a refreshing exploration of contemporary contributions by psychologists to problems of social change. While their work is by no means exhaustive, Jeffrey Travers and Stuart Pizer invite us to consider wide-ranging points of social leverage. They avoid the bias of premature commitment to a single means for change, and they are careful not to lay down an unwarranted blueprint for what society must become. They do not burst forth with the optimism of the uninitiated, but instead carefully select several promising routes toward change, and document both their advantages and shortcomings. The volume moves from a focus on change within the single individual to change in our major institutions and cultural traditions. After an initial consideration of individual psychotherapy the focus is shifted to group encounter and sensitivity training. From the small group, we then move to a pointed discussion of our prison systems and mental institutions. Social change is no less based on techniques for modification than on probing assessments of the effects of current practices. As the authors demonstrate, in the realm of penology and mental health our current practices leave much to be desired. The discussion is rounded out by an incisive inquiry into contemporary socialization practices. Comparing our practices, particularly in the realm of education, with those employed in other nations, makes us aware that we are left with serious questions for the future.

The authors of the volume are ideally suited to the task they have undertaken. Both hold Ph.D. degrees from Harvard's Department of Social Relations. Pizer has spent innumerable hours in conducting self-analytic groups; he wrote his dissertation on the efficacy of such groups in promoting personal change. Since that time he has served as a psychotherapist at the Harvard University Health Services, where he directs training in group therapy and couples therapy. Jeffrey Travers combined his graduate work in social and developmental psychology with a consulting practice that enabled him to study current penal practices. He has since been teaching psychology at Swarthmore College, where he has had prime responsibility for the curriculum in child development, and has made a major input into both cognitive and educational psychology. As editor for this series, it has been a pure pleasure for me to work with these very gifted individuals. The reader should find equal pleasure in their work—although their message is far from comforting.

Kenneth J. Gergen
Professor and Chairman
Department of Psychology
Swarthmore College

Acknowledgments

We feel gratitude for many sources of encouragement, support, and insight as we labored on this volume.

Dr. Kenneth Gergen, who initiated this book, has played a special role in our beginnings in the field of psychology. We thank him for his patience as our editor.

Mrs. Kayla Freedman Bernheim and Dr. Gordon Carr contributed advice concerning mental hospitals and provided an opportunity to study one firsthand. Abt Associates, Inc., made possible our participation in a research project on prisons and their aftereffects.

Dr. Barbara Massar has generously agreed to our use of the case study in Chapter 3 that grew out of her colleagueship (with Stuart Pizer) in the Human Relations Seminar. Mrs. Marcia Erozer assisted with acumen in our preparation of the manuscript.

Eva Travers has given her moral support and good advice.

The authors wish to acknowledge here the following material used with permission from other sources:

Childhood and Society, revised, 2nd ed., by Erik H. Erikson, Copyright 1950, © 1963, W. W. Norton and Co. Inc.

Warren Bennis and Herbert Shepard, "A Theory of Group Development," *Human Relations,* 9:4, 1956.

Eugene Gendlin, "A Theory of Personality Change," in Philip Worchel and Don Byrne (eds.), *Personality Change* © 1964, John Wiley & Sons, Inc.

R. D. Laing, *The Divided Self,* Tavistock Publications, 1965.

Carl Rogers, "The Process of the Basic Encounter Group," in James Bugental (ed.), *Challenges of Humanistic Psychology,* McGraw-Hill Book Co., 1967.

Stuart A. Pizer
Jeffrey R. Travers

Chapter 1

Introduction

It was the best of times, it was the worst of times, it was the age of wisdom, it was the age of foolishness, it was the epoch of belief, it was the epoch of incredulity, it was the season of Light, it was the season of Darkness, it was the spring of hope, it was the winter of despair, we had everything before us, we had nothing before us, we were all going direct to Heaven, we were all going direct the other way....

Charles Dickens

Dickens could well be writing about the current state of American society as seen in our contemporary media. He has captured perfectly the apocalyptic, and contradictory, tone of a flood of magazine and Sunday supplement articles. One author tells us we are all hurtling meteorically through social changes that leave us future-shocked, revolutionized, and unrested. Another author protests the elephantine sluggishness of social change, reminding us that you can't teach an old dog, or a "fat cat," new tricks.

What are we to believe, or understand, in all this? Is America now in the throes of vast social change, or is ours a stagnant society? Signs of change are all around us, but it is hard to tell which, if any, point the way to important alterations in the way we live. Obvious, well-publicized events may be irrelevant for truly fundamental change, while crucial happenings may go unnoticed because they lack publicity value, or because their long-range importance is not grasped. Phenomena that seem to betoken social upheaval leap at us from the news: the generation gap, the sexual revolution, radical politics, the militance of blacks and other minorities, women's liberation, gay liberation, communal families, and so on and on. Yet, at the same time, researchers tell us that, on the whole, basic values and attitudes of children continue to reflect those of their parents, that the sexual behavior of today's young is not as different from earlier generations as we have been led to believe. Similarly, conservatives and radicals alike hold that the emphasis of the media on radical activism is misleading: conservatives argue that advocates of radical change represent only a tiny, disgruntled minority and that most blacks, women, and citizens in general are content with things as they are, or desire changes quite different from those proposed by the "agitators." Radicals counter that the media emphasize the superficial and sensational—confrontations between antiwar demonstrators and the police, bra-burning at the Miss America pageant—while the deeper issues behind the actions remain ignored. The media, they say, create the illusion that change is occurring, while in reality the oppression of racial minorities, labor, women, the young, etc., continues unabated. Where is the substance and where is the shadow in all this confusion? And how can psychology help to clarify the issues, to identify the changes that are likely to be of enduring significance, and, perhaps most important, to help realize change for the better?

As psychologists, we would like to think that psychology can help us to understand and promote societal change in several ways:

First, it can help us to discern the *need* for change, by pointing out the kinds of psychological problems that existing social arrangements create for individuals. For example, black psychologists Kenneth and Mamie Clark helped bring to public attention the damaging effects of segregated schools on the self-images of black children (Clark & Clark, 1947, 1950). Their testimony influenced the 1954 Supreme Court desegregation decision.

Second, psychology can help us estimate both the costs and benefits of alternative kinds of change. Again the situation of black children in the schools provides an example: some spokesmen argue that racial integration is the only remedy for the inequalities of school systems that are both white-dominated and segregated, by law or by the consequence of residential patterns. On the other hand, advocates of community control hold that racial homogeneity in itself is tolerable—if black parents control their children's schools. By studying children in integrated and community-controlled schools psychologists can help spell out the effects of the two arrangements on the academic achievement, motivation, and self-concepts of the children involved.

Third, psychology can help provide the *means* for change. Many of the obstacles to social change are psychological in nature—values, attitudes, fantasies, fears, and behaviors that need to be altered. Psychology, we hope, can contribute to social change by helping us understand what is entailed in the process of change, by offering viable intervention techniques, and by providing men and women trained as clinicians, social researchers, and other types of change agents, whose field of expertise is the improvement of human relationships.

Having outlined, rather optimistically, some ways in which psychology is relevant to the broadest kinds of social change, we must also make clear some of its limitations:

First, psychology by itself can never tell us what to do. It can help us to understand our alternatives, but it cannot dictate our choice among them. Values and politics inevitably play a role in social choices. For example, no matter what the psychologist may discover about the pros and cons of integrated or community-controlled schools, the decision on which course to pursue is not his to make. Psychological facts alone do not determine what action should be taken.

Second, it would be arrogant of psychologists to presume that they are simply expert observers and directors of social change. Psychologists are also the products of social change, with *their* consciousness structured by social conditions and social changes. Thus, a psychologist's personal values partially determine what problems he studies, and, perhaps inevitably, affect his findings to some degree as well.

Third, psychologists simply are not omniscient and omnipotent. They are constantly consulted for expert opinions, judgments, and explanations of social events for which existing knowledge provides no definitive understanding. More significantly, they are sought for immediate solutions to complex social problems. And, the pain of individuals will not wait for the accretion of psychological wisdom or certitude. Psychologists are subject to the compelling demands of the suffering and oppressed, and are also vulnerable to the seductive proffers of the empowered and oppressive. Psychologists must remain aware that sometimes Necessity is the mother of fabrication, and that, as psychologists, we can promise "no easy victories" (to borrow John Gardner's phrase).

Even further, we must remind ourselves that since utopias based on deliberate social control can turn hellishly totalitarian, it is encumbent upon psychologists to temper their insights with responsibility. In the chapters that follow we shall consider the *practical* issues of social change, utilizing the insights and methods derived from psychological theory and research. It is our hope that throughout our exploration we, and our readers, will not lose sight of the intrinsic *ethical* issues of choice and responsibility.

We wish to put to rest the notion that psychologists serve the insidious conservative function of "adjusting" individuals to intolerable social conditions, thus deflecting the thrust of social reforms. Our impression of the radically caricatured psychologist is that he serves as society's sanitation department at the same time that he offers individuals the decadent service of "interior design." We do recognize the argument that the psychologist is a specialist in working with individuals or small groups, and that the pursuit of broader avenues of social change are beyond his professional competence. Further, it could be asserted that many cases of personal maladjustment may be more the fault of society than of the individual involved. For example, an energetic woman may feel frustrated and depressed in her role as a housewife, or a talented black person may experience similar feelings when confined to a job beneath his abilities. But the psychologist is not simply a person who enters the picture to help this man or woman passively accept his or her lot. As we shall elaborate in Chapter 2, even for the clinical psychologist, or psychiatrist, who focuses his efforts at the individual level, the goal of psychological intervention is not simply individual adaptation and apathy.

Through psychotherapy the individual may come to assume greater *responsibility* in his own life. And, taking the word "responsibility" quite literally, we would emphasize that treatment for the individual may help increase his ability to respond constructively and effectively; that is, he will not be merely the passive victim of external events and of his own feelings. Thus, the individual's capacity to take such responsibility in his life entails freedom from being coerced, misled, or tyrannized by sources both outside him and within him. Hence, the psychological processes through which an individual may discern the actual extent of his personal power can afford him some liberation within his social context. It is our bias that as the individual increases his own personal *integration* his judicious indignation (to paraphrase Erik Erikson) and his creative insight can be more realistically mobilized for autonomous action in and upon his social environment.

Finally, we submit that the psychological integration of the individual should be conceived as an ideal goal or value. It is a state that can never be fully achieved, and the degree to which it can be approached is profoundly affected by the social milieu in which the individual lives. At the same time, however, it is a state that is consistent with a person's membership in a wide range of social systems, or with his subscription to a diversity of political ideologies.

Thus, according to our view, psychotherapy for a Lenin would not constitute an effort to dispel his revolutionary ideology, but an effort at sharpening his awareness of the personal wellsprings that inform and impel his actions in the world. An integrated man is one who does take a stand, who knows where he stands, and who does not assume his stand is "for free." He is willing to pay the prices of his own responsible adult choices. And further, his responsibility or ability to respond effectively and judiciously implies an ability to perceive conditions as they exist, both around him and within him.

How, concretely, can a psychologist take action in the service of the goals we have outlined? From our earlier examples of the frustrated housewife and the overqualified black man, we can discern a number of avenues: a clinician might engage such people in individual psychotherapy, possibly resulting in their fuller understanding of how their social situations have produced apparently unconnected, yet troubling and destructive, patterns of feeling and behavior. Alternatively, the woman and her husband might enter a couples therapy group in order to explore more fully the nature of their relationship and its potential for change. Or a psychologist might act as a human relations consultant for the business firm employing the overqualified black; in such a capacity he might help management and employees to see the psychological consequences of racial discrimination on the job, and to find ways of alleviating the situation. Or, psychologists might contribute more basically to the solution of the problems of race and sex stereotypes by working within educational institutions in an effort to find ways to counter the perpetuation of cultural biases in children.

Thus, it is clear that there are a variety of ways and settings in which psychologists can approach problems of social change. Each of these raises its own theoretical, practical, and ethical issues. We have tried to conceptualize and simplify this multiplicity of endeavor by speaking of change at four levels: that of the individual, the group, the institution, and society itself. These four levels determine the organization of chapters in the present volume.

This book is a circle. We begin by looking, with a clinician's eye, at personality change in individuals. We then move on to examine the interactions between individuals in their social relationships in face-to-face groups. We then proceed to an elaboration of the complex relationships of individuals organized and guided in the larger social groupings called institutions, particularly institutions designed to produce specific forms of change. Finally, we explore those patterns of a society and culture that give form to the life of its members. We shall see that any action or change at any point in the social system can reverberate throughout the system, and is significant precisely in terms of its impact upon individuals. Indeed, as the sociologists Talcott Parsons and Edward Shils (Parsons & Shils, 1951) have observed, the social system is made up of the relationships of individuals, and social change is internalized by individuals as personality change. Thus, we will have come full circle in our exposition of change in the complex, interpenetrating systems of personality and society.

Psychology is concerned with processes in the individual; therefore, as we devote separate chapters of this book to change in individuals, groups, institutions, and society, our focus remains on the individual. We treat small groups as environments in which individuals sharpen their insights into group processes and into their own motives. Our discussion of institutions is highly selective; we focus on prisons and mental hospitals, two forms of establishment through which society tries to bring about change in two types of deviants—lawbreakers and the mentally ill. Our discussion of change at the societal level focuses on socialization and society's attempt to stabilize, regenerate, and modify itself by shaping the values and loyalties of children.

Our focus on the individual is determined by our profession. We do not mean to imply that all social change must begin with individuals, nor to deny that change in individuals is often predicated upon changes in broader social or economic structures. For example, we concede that changes in the technology of production, or in systems of ownership and control of productive resources, may have profound effects on individual human potential. Nevertheless we maintain that the psychological concomitants of such change are important to study in their own right, and that change at the individual level can have rippling effects on social and economic structures as well. In Chapter 3, for example, we will discuss a bold attempt to stimulate economic growth in developing nations by direct transformation of the motives of entrepreneurs in a small group context. In short, we are not arguing for a single direction of causality, from psychological to social change, but for an interplay of changes at each level.

We have omitted from this volume consideration of many important issues. In part, we felt the need to select single illustrative aspects of societal change for discussion—those broad enough to touch on a wide range of contemporary concerns, yet narrow enough to ᴗe outlined in a treatment of this length and depth. Certain topics, appropriate in scope and importance, were set aside because they are treated in far more detail in other texts in this series on psychology and problems of society. In particular, contemporary changes in race relations are covered in *The Psychology of Intergroup Conflict,* by Phillip Brickman, Louise Kidder, and Mary Stewart. Urbanization and urban decay are covered in Richard Ashmore and John McConohay's *Psychology and America's Urban Dilemma.* Political activism is treated in Stanley Morse's *Psychology of Political Action.* And Russell Eisenman devotes a volume to *Psychology and Social Deviance.* As much as possible, we have tried to concentrate on aspects of social change that are distinct from those covered in the other volumes so as to keep overlap to a minimum.

Other major societal issues are excluded from this volume on psychology and social change because psychologists have just begun to enter the fray on these social fronts. Population growth and ecology are significant examples. Psychologists are now attempting to augment our understanding of the relationship between man and environment—for example, why families continue to make their homes in cyclone corridors, or why a tribe chooses to live on the treacherous and unfertile slope of a mountain, or why some societies reproduce in greater numbers than their food supply can support, or what it is about a landscape or a building that provokes feelings of loneliness and alienation, or why people stubbornly ignore the sober warnings of urban blight and species extinction. This work remains for the future.

Finally, we have excluded from our discussion many timely and profound issues precisely because of their timeliness. While significant problems, such as the relations between the races and sexes, will be with us for years to come, many specific manifestations of those broad concerns will change rapidly with the immediate historical situation. For example, it was less than a decade ago that voter registration in the rural South was *the* central event in race relations, and only months ago (as of this writing) that protest against the Vietnam war was *the* central focus of student radicalism. It is our hope to deal in this book with the more fundamental psychological processes in social change that will endure despite constant historical shifts in the concrete focus of change.

Chapter 2

Psychology and Change in Individuals

At the dawn of this century, Sigmund Freud provided us with a new psychological technique, which Erik H. Erikson has described as a means of "cure-research," a new way to engage in treatment and investigation through the power of a personal relationship. The psychoanalytic method of inner exploration and personal change has yielded as well a potentially significant catalyst for vital social change.

The growth of psychoanalytic psychiatry has also eventually led to the emergence of other modes of individual psychotherapy based on various psychological theories of personality and personality change. Aside from behavior therapy—which we shall consider later in this chapter—all the significant varieties of psychotherapy are based on some combination of a personal relationship, a feeling process, and insight. Whether existential analysis, client-centered therapy, gestalt, transactional, or eclectic, each has in common with psychoanalysis (despite the disguises assumed in the argot of each group) a personal relationship that focuses on the wholeness of what a person experiences, consciously or otherwise; the internal world and the external world; anxiety and defense; rationality and emotion; the residues of past experiences; and insight. Each major school of therapy recognizes a set of ethics about human relationships that values growth and development, honesty and trust, acceptance and caring confrontation, and the integrity of persons.

Freud certainly merits a place in the "great man" theory of history along with those special individuals whose singular lives have catalyzed momentous social change. The implications of Freud's broad social theories will be considered in Chapter 5. However, it is Freud's impact upon the lives of individuals, and upon our psychological understanding of the lives of individuals, that warrants our attention here. Since Freud established the essentials of psychiatric practice, the multitude of individuals who have undertaken a personal psychotherapy, analytic or otherwise, has included among its numbers great and powerful people. It is tempting to speculate on the effect on social change implicit in the undertaking of psychotherapy by political, artistic, professional, intellectual, and perhaps even military leaders. A case in point (Jones, 1963, pp. 271-72): In 1910, the great German composer Gustav Mahler sought a consultation with Freud, who was vacationing on the Baltic Coast. Mahler apparently suffered from an obsessional neurosis and was disturbed by impotence in his relationship with his wife Alma. Freud agreed to interrupt his vacation enough to offer an appointment to Mahler. They met at a hotel in Leyden and conducted a four-hour perambulatory "analysis," wandering through the streets of the town. (It is noteworthy that the "father of psychoanalysis" was so capable of unorthodox methods in what was perhaps the first marathon session. The analytic couch, the fifty-minute hour, the unseen analyst, the working-through of a "transference" were evidently not such invariants to Freud as they seem to have become to the less flexible and creative latter-day Freudians.) During their four-hour session, Freud explored Mahler's relationship with his dominating mother, Marie Mahler, and his subsequent responses to his wife Alma Maria (called Marie), the daughter of a painter (in German "Mahler").

Not only did this conversation alleviate the composer's marital complaints, but Mahler was suddenly able to recognize "why his music had always been prevented from achieving the highest rank." It had been characteristic of Mahler's music that the noble and rhapsodic were interposed with the common and banal. He had never managed to integrate his melodic and tonal creativity with his penchant for folk themes and pop effects. Rather, in his symphonies a sophisticated and poignantly emotional passage would be interrupted by the intrusion of a trite popular tune. With Freud's help, Mahler explored his childhood family situation, particularly his father's brutality and abuse of his mother. Mahler recalled to awareness an especially painful episode between his parents when he became overwhelmed by the unbearable emotional pitch and raced outside the house. There, in the street to which the young boy fled, a hurdy-gurdy was playing the popular Viennese tune, "Ach, Du lieber Augustin." Recalling this moment, Mahler then understood how "the conjunction of high tragedy and light amusement" had become inextricably fused in his mind, leading to his musical signature of deep emotion which triggered a leap to the burlesque. Thus, four hours spent in the presence of Freud by a great composer held promise of profound changes in the course of music history.

Assuredly, such meteoric results are not common in psychotherapy. Nor does individual psychotherapy commonly yield benefits so clearly translatable into a socially visible harvest. Nevertheless, psychotherapy and psychoanalysis are today widely available, and many persons with important roles in society—and members of their families—have been in therapy. Clearly, psychotherapists have been in a position to help shape social values and social events through the often profound impact of their intimate work with influential individuals.

Moreover, the dual cure-research aspects of dynamic psychotherapy apply fundamentally to broad programs of extensive social change. After all, no matter how vast a project is designed by social engineers, no matter how huge its budget or implementary bureaucratic machinery, or how large the target population, any effort to transform, develop, or elevate people necessitates change in individuals. This is simple reality: the cutting edge of social change works at the level of the individual. Social change is change in an aggregate of individuals. Any effort at deliberate social reform will founder to the extent that it fails to appreciate and accommodate the basic processes of change in the social units of personality and interpersonal relationship. To this end, the cure-research of dynamic psychotherapy contributes a means of intervention and investigation.

WHAT IS PSYCHOTHERAPY?

There are so many myths, fantasies, and dogmas regarding the nature of psychotherapy—each claiming the imprimatur of reality—that some discussion of this question is essential. Indeed, within the profession the case is far from closed. Psychotherapy has been variously represented as the *science* of behavior shaping and thought control or the *art* of human interaction (White, 1964, p. 318). It has been characterized by its medical origins, implying *cure* through the laying on of hands. It has been typified in movies and magazine caricatures by the bald-headed, middle-European Svengalis with hypnotic powers and lip-smacking pruriencies. The position taken here is that psychotherapy is a form of treatment, but not something that a doctor *does to* a patient. Psychotherapy reflects a science based on hypotheses, empirical evidence in the clinic, research, and standards of conduct, but not a fact-based framework for the control of behavior. It is a creative process shared by two people, but not such an ineffable will-o'-the-wisp as can be captured and described only through artful metaphors. Psychotherapy is a simple human collaboration, a working alliance, and not a mystical or decadent indulgence.

And, despite the orthodoxies of discrete schools of thought that delineate certain artifacts as the sine qua non of psychotherapy (e.g., the couch in psychoanalysis or bodily action in gestalt therapy), there is a growing recognition, and important substantiating research, for the basic commonalities in the therapeutic process when it is working. Indeed, Freud's willingness to improvise with Mahler bears testimony to the first psychoanalyst's wisdom in this regard. Leo Tolstoy wrote, at the beginning of *Anna Karenina*, "Happy families are all alike; every unhappy family is unhappy in its own way." What Tolstoy says about the happiness of families might be said about the effectiveness of psychotherapy.

The Conditions of Psychotherapy

Carl R. Rogers (1967) and Eugene T. Gendlin (1964) have ventured a theory of therapeutic process supported by years of research effort. Gendlin cites as support for a universal model of therapeutic process previous research studies on the outcome of therapy. All these studies generally indicate the same success rate—approximately 60 percent—no matter what school of technique was employed. Other research, according to Gendlin (1962, p. 261), has found "much more similarity between experienced therapists of *different* schools than between experienced and inexperienced therapists of the *same* school." The factors considered by Rogers and Gendlin to be vital for psychotherapeutic effectiveness are not the explicit tenets of training and theory but qualities of the therapist as a person: namely, "congruence," "unconditional positive regard," and "empathic understanding."

Congruence The most basic of the three conditions for successful psychotherapy, therapist congruence refers to the degree to which the therapist exists in the therapeutic encounter as an integrated and genuine person. Congruence is the most basic factor because conceptual understanding or respect for the patient conveyed by a therapist in a hollow, superficial, rehearsed, or unconvinced way offers small help and cold comfort indeed. Hence, the therapist must not be putting up a front (e.g., of experience, knowledge, magic, or caring), playing a role, or maintaining a polite, professional façade. Rogers and Truax (in Rogers, 1967, p. 100) emphasize the need for "transparency" in the therapist, a quality of "openly being the feelings and attitudes which at the moment are flowing in him." The therapist must be aware of what he himself is feeling, and not denying himself. Yet, his expression of his own experience in the therapeutic moment must also take into account the current needs of the patient. It is understandable that Harry Stack Sullivan (1953) described the psychotherapist as "an expert in human relations."

This openness and transparency on the part of the therapist is not a willy-nilly disclosure of any-or-all feelings. It is not a burdening of the client with everything that comes to the therapist's mind. And certainly it is not an imposition of the therapist's personal worries, an unloading of his problems upon the patient (such an occurrence is probably a form of malpractice). Rather, the congruent, or genuine, therapist is aware of his continuous and complex flow of experiencing, and able to use his feelings constructively. For example, a therapist may become aware that he is feeling bored during a therapy session and, rather than contriving, wittingly or unwittingly, some attribution to the patient (e.g., "You certainly are a boring person"), he uses his feelings to help clarify the blockages in the current therapist-patient interaction (e.g., "I feel like you're holding me at a distance today with small talk"). The therapist might, if he believes it has value, go on to ask the patient, "Is it your intention to put me off?" It may turn out that the patient is, in fact, angry with him, or feeling mistrustful. Or, if the therapist recalls that the patient had touched upon some sources of anxiety at their previous session, the therapist might go on to ask, "Do you feel like backing off from strong feelings today?" It is apparent that much therapeutic mileage could be lost if the therapist were unaware of his feeling of boredom at that moment, if he did not give his feelings credence, or if he were unable to own up to his feelings undefensively. A therapist who is sensitive to, and comfortable with, only some of his feelings is, to that degree, hampered in his effectiveness. Rogers does not discuss prerequisite training for psychotherapists, but within the psychoanalytic tradition it is customary (and, for membership in any psychoanalytic institute, mandatory) to undertake a training analysis in order to develop as an integrated and genuine person, able to be congruent in his interpersonal relationships.

Unconditional Positive Regard One feeling a therapist must be genuinely aware of, according to Rogers, is his prizing of the client. A good therapist will not keep in treatment a patient for whom he does not feel a genuine caring uncontaminated by his evaluations of the patient's behavior. The therapist must experience "a non-possessive caring for the client as a separate person" (1967, p. 103). Rogers does not mean having a paternalistic, sentimental, or superficially agreeable attitude. Indeed, a saccharine tolerance for any-and-all outrageous, hurtful, or antisocial behavior would be an inadequate expression of a therapist's genuine caring. Rather, the therapist implicitly says to his patient, "I am willing to bear with, stay with, and work with this awful thing you have done, or this awful feeling you have." The therapist's inclination must be to understand and not to judge, to foster a spirit of self-inquiry and not to cut off personal exploration by evaluating or rejecting the patient, although he may clearly indicate that he does not personally condone a particular asocial act.

The therapist must be comfortable with his own genuine wishes to nurture the patient. He must be able to sustain his recognition of the good in a patient who is presently confronting him with unpleasantness. As the patient grows increasingly aware that his therapist's acceptance and prizing of him as a person is not conditional or transient, he experiences a "safe" environment in which to explore himself and a human relationship whereby he can feel deeply engaged.

Accurate Empathic Understanding The therapist conveys his regard for the patient through his effort to understand the meaning of the patient's feelings and experiences. This is the *work* of therapy that transpires in a contextual relationship of genuineness and caring.

The two aspects of accurate empathic understanding suggested by Rogers are (1) *perceptive* and (2) *communicative*. The therapist must be able to apprehend the patient's inner world and feel what it is like to have that person's perspective. The therapist must sense what his patient feels as if these were his own feelings—without losing sight of the "as if." In other words, the therapist must be comfortably at home in the patient's "mother tongue." Such empathic understanding must be immediately conveyed to be of use to the patient. Whatever understanding the therapist arrives at after the session has little value for the patient unless another occasion spontaneously arises to communicate it. Empathic understanding entails the communication of insight at the experiential moment that is ripe for the patient. In this way, the therapist most succinctly says "I am with you" and helps the patient to arrive at a more clear sense or formulation of the *meaning* in his immediate experience.

By the very act of attending carefully to the meaning of what his patient says (verbally and nonverbally) the therapist is affirming that "your feelings and meanings are *worth* understanding." He fosters a spirit of self-exploration, and models an attitude of active listening.

Rogers further elaborates the quality of empathic understanding by indicating what it is not. A low level of empathic understanding is manifested if the therapist goes off on his own tangent, holds doggedly onto a misinterpretation, preoccupies himself with his own intellectual interpretations, indulges his own idiosyncratic language, or focuses exclusively on the content of what the patient says. To Rogers' exposition, it might be added that any rigidity of thinking or interacting on the part of the therapist that restricts his openness to the patient's unique "being" is evidence of diminished empathy. Any conceptual monotony, such as the therapist's pet theory, that is superimposed as a stencil on the therapeutic relationship will interfere with the flexibility of accurate empathic understanding. Hence, any excessive, imbalanced, or unyielding focus on content *or* process, past *or* present, will prove insensitive to the patient's full experiential reality. Any such rigidity on the patient's part would be considered a form of *resistance* by psychoanalysts (Greenson, 1967), and the therapist must take responsibility for his own resistance to aspects or implications of his patient's feelings. Further, a psychotherapist ought not to convey his insight by condescending, manipulating, or explaining the patient to himself with a teacher-pupil flavor.

The Process of Psychotherapy

Eugene Gendlin has gone beyond Rogers' description of the qualities of a psychotherapist to explicate the process of personality change in psychotherapy. And it is worth reminding ourselves that the primary unit of social change is personality change. In his essay "A Theory of Personality Change" (1964), Gendlin argues that psychotherapy consists of a *personal relationship* and a *feeling process.* The personal relationship is facilitated by the conditions of effective therapy just described. It is Gendlin's articulation of the feeling process that furthers our understanding of therapeutic change in individuals.

According to Gendlin, the focus of personality change is change in the process of experiencing. Gendlin describes the characteristics of the experiencing process as follows:

1 Experiencing is *felt,* rather than thought, known, or verbalized.

2 Experiencing occurs *in the immediate present;* it does not consist of generalized attributes of a person such as traits, complexes, or dispositions; rather, experiencing is what a person feels here and now, in each moment. Hence, experiencing is a changing flow of feelings.

3 Experiencing can be *directly referred to:* it provides a *direct referent,* a concretely felt meaning, which is evident when a person says, "I have this feeling inside—I can't explain it yet, but I know it's there."

4 Experiencing, as it is directly referred to, is *implicitly meaningful* and *guides conceptualization.* This is the basis for self-exploration. That is, experiencing is a process by which new meanings are created as undifferentiated feelings become clarified in a person's awareness. For example, a person's initial sense that "I have this vague feeling of uneasiness that I can't quite put into words" ... can give way to "I'm scared to face his judgment." And the initial implicit meaning ("this

vague feeling of uneasiness") can be directly referred to once again to measure the accuracy of the new conceptualization ("I'm scared to face his judgment"). At this point, the person might say, "Yes, that's what I'm feeling"; or, he might say, "No ... now that's not quite it ... I'm not feeling just that. It's more that I *resent* all these times I get judged."

Therapeutic change occurs through a process Gendlin calls *focusing*. Essentially, focusing is "the whole process which ensues when the individual attends to the direct referent of experiencing" (see example above). Focusing in psychotherapy seems to consist of four discernible phases.

Direct Reference (Phase One of Focusing) When a patient directly refers to what he definitely feels, he senses that "I am in touch with myself." It may be that the felt meaning is conceptually vague, yet it is distinctly felt. The therapist encourages the patient to focus his attention on this direct referent, and not to break off attending to it because it seems too foolish, or too bad, or too unclear. If the patient does not hasten to intellectually explain, defend, or justify himself, he may become able to conceptualize some rough aspects of what he has vaguely apprehended. For example, he may find: "I sense this kind of dread only with certain people." Having conceptualized some rough aspect of this feeling, which was initially sensed as some vague "it," the patient usually feels this felt meaning more intensely and vividly. He becomes excited and hopeful about continuing the process of focusing. It is like coming home to himself.

This direct referent may continue to be mostly vague, just "this feeling." Conceptually it may be unclear. But nothing is vague about the way the patient *feels* it—like a lump in the middle of himself. It is inwardly sensed, and quite present in the immediate moment.

Gendlin has observed that when a patient attends directly to this inner felt referent he becomes less tense and anxious. Even if the content or topic under exploration is an anxiety-laden or uncomfortable matter, discomfort actually *decreases* as the patient moves closer to the direct referent. Gendlin's explanation is that it is intrinsically relieving for a person to find the meaning of what he is implicitly experiencing. He feels suddenly unstuck. He can carry forward the natural process of feeling and the creation of personal meaning.

Unfolding (Phase Two of Focusing) As Gendlin writes:

> Sometimes, in focusing on a directly felt referent, there is a gradual step-by-step process of coming to know explicitly what it is. Yet, it may "open up" in one dramatic instant. . . . With a great physical relief and sudden dawning, the individual suddenly knows. He may sit there, nodding to himself, thinking only words such as "Yes, I've got it" quite without as yet finding concepts to tell himself what it is he "has got." However, he knows that now he *can* say. (Gendlin, 1964, p. 118)

At this moment, an insensitive or unempathizing therapist might interrupt him with an irrelevant remark, and the patient may "lose it," whereby later he can only say, "I really sensed that I knew what I felt at that moment, but I've lost it now." However, with a timely remark (or by simply staying out of the patient's way!) the therapist may help his patient swiftly find concepts and words to say what has opened up. Almost always, "this feeling" that was felt as just *one thing* turns out to be a *number of things*. The sense of "it" becomes a more explicit experiencing of multiplicity. For example, as one patient might say:

> Yes, *of course* I've been refusing to listen to the white people in my class. That's behind the feeling I've had of tensing up and withdrawing when I walk in there and see them. I haven't permitted myself to even think about this going on, let alone deal with it. Well, yes, I always did realize it was going on—but I always blamed them . . . like, they haven't been through what I been through, they're just different. And, it was always partly my fear of them judging me . . . not listening to what I have to say. But . . . now . . . it's also I don't want to hear from them. I hear them say things that I can sort of identify with. Only I haven't wanted to hear that. I keep saying to myself "We're *not* the same, so don't listen!" But, shit, if I'm that mad, then it's even worse. I mean, what if I don't give anyone—myself—a chance? But, at least it's a relief to know that's what it's been.

This example illustrates the rich and complex multiplicity that unfolds as the patient refers directly to what he had felt as one "this" (for example, "this tenseness"). Also, it is noteworthy in our example that although the problem is not at all resolved, the patient feels relieved.

Indeed, the situation now seems *worse,* even deeper. Yet, the unfolding of a direct referent always produces tension reduction. Now it seems clear to the person why he has felt tense. He experiences a surprising and deeply emotional recognition of the good sense of his own feelings. He feels tempted to exclaim, "Of course!" or "So that's it!" As Gendlin asserts, "because what was previously felt now actually 'makes sense', problem resolutions can occur at this stage" (1964, p. 119).

Such problem resolutions may result from an awareness that "given this perception of white people, of course I've reacted that way—but now I see them different." But, it is more than a mere conceptual realization that has taken place. At the next therapy hour the patient may report that his whole feeling of the problem has already changed, and even his behavior is different. And his only explanation may be "Well, it just feels different now; it just seems O.K." There has been "a global change in the whole manner of experiencing in this regard" (Gendlin, 1964, p. 119).

Global Application (Phase Three of Focusing) Gendlin writes:

> This global way in which the process of direct reference and unfolding affects many aspects of the person is noticeable not only in his later reports of the resulting difference, but also in the moments which immediately follow the unfolding of a felt referent. The individual is flooded by many different associations, memories, situations, and circumstances, all in relation to the felt referent. Although conceptually they can be very different, they share the same felt meaning with which he has been dealing. Except for this they may concern quite different and unrelated matters. (Gendlin, 1964, p. 120)

It is as if a felt-tip marker were used to connect a network of cities on a map: "Oh, and that's also why I avoided taking those other classes." "Yes, and another thing about it is, this feeling hits me every time someone else says something I have also felt. I can't say I agree, because then this fear of not being different comes in." "Oh, wow! Also, that's just what was going on in high school. The time when 'this' and 'this' happened. It was the same feeling then." Many of these new connections may be given utterance by the patient, and in psychotherapy it is this event that is generally termed *insight.* But this process of global application may also occur as the patient sits silently. Indeed, as Gendlin points out, "One can be sure that for every relation or application the individual here explicitly thinks, there are thousands which he does not think of, but which have, nevertheless, just changed" (1964, p. 120). Thus, Gendlin's model of personality change in psychotherapy covers not only "the return of the repressed," the new recollection of past traumas, but also a profound realignment of the patient's whole manner of experiencing.

Referent Movement (Phase Four of Focusing) Once a patient has referred to and named what has hitherto been only vaguely felt, and once he has discerned the more global connections of the feeling he has named, he finds that he now refers to "a direct referent which feels different." The person has now arrived at the next level in a cascade of feelings. According to Gendlin, "the *implicit* meanings which he can symbolize from this direct referent are now quite different ones." With this new direct referent, the four-phase focusing process begins again, propelling a continuous flow of experiencing. And now, the "scenery" the patient encounters in his exploration has changed.

The process of focusing in psychotherapy could be visualized roughly in terms of an endless series of oceans linked by an endless string of canals. From one vast sea of feelings a certain portion is admitted into a first "lock," and named. This volume of experienced feeling is then passed along and channeled through all the subdivisions of connected meanings until it flows out into a new sea at a lower level. Entry into this new ocean of feelings marks the phase of *referent movement,* and direct reference can once again provide a new canal to carry forward the ongoing process of experiencing. Gendlin has observed that psychotherapy consists essentially of *reconstituting* an individual's experiencing process when it has become stuck at any of the four phases.

Critics of Traditional Psychotherapy

Some critics of psychotherapy argue that this process of exploring feelings leads the individual to a state of complacency, contentment with a status quo, or adjustment to injustices in the environment. Such critics contend that a certain level of frustration or anger may be necessary for a person to participate in protest marches, sit-ins, or strikes; they fear that the release of personal tensions may reduce a person's motivation to engage in social action. However, it should be apparent at this point that an empathic relationship in psychotherapy can help a person tap into his own sources of strength and discern the extent of his personal power. Further, at moments of global application and referent movement in therapy new options for action become apparent to the individual. More vividly aware of the network "mapped out" in his experienced world, the person may assume greater freedom to make informed and autonomous choices. Psychotherapy can lead to the potential not only for new conceptual insights but also for new courses of action-in-the-world.

Other critics of psychotherapy contend that this process of personality change is too ineffable, too undemonstrable, or too unverifiable to trust as a medically or scientifically valid procedure. A key statement among these critics is H. J. Eysenck's (1961) survey of research studies of therapeutic improvement in neurotic adults. Eysenck presents the recovery rate for patients treated psychoanalytically as 44 percent; in other eclectic treatments it is 64 percent. He compares these rates with a 72 percent recovery rate in another study for spontaneous improvement in *untreated* individuals. Comparing these relative rates of improvement, Eysenck concludes that the outcome of psychotherapy reflects a lower rate of recovery than no psychotherapy at all! Conclusions of this kind seem irresponsibly hasty in a study comparing populations of patients who were not matched for pathology, age, socioeconomic background, etc. However, it is also true that very little published data present strong positive *statistical* evidence in favor of the efficacy of psychotherapy.

A further shortcoming of Eysenck's study, which impels us to doubt his results, is the use of different, and probably noncomparable, criteria for measuring successful outcomes of treatment. In the various patient populations, patient reports of self-esteem or self-awareness are compared with outcome results based on therapists' opinions. And the criterion for successful outcome in the untreated group is the person's demonstrated capacity, after a work disability, to avoid a recurrence of work disability for another five years. This is like the proverbial comparison of "apples and oranges"—a ridiculous research approach, and hardly a reliable basis for impugning the reliability of psychotherapy. Brendan Maher has written succinctly on this general dilemma of defining adequate criteria for improvement against which to measure the adequacy of various psychological treatments:

> Generally speaking, we may look for evidence of some behavioral change in the direction of effectiveness, some change in expressions of distress in the direction of greater comfort, or some change in the patient's account of his problems in the direction of greater awareness or "insight." Many workers use these three criteria in a global or total fashion, assuming implicitly that they are all representative of some single general process of improvement. (Maher, 1966, p. 471)

Maher then cites a careful study of change in patients in which measurements of all these various outcome criteria, taken on all patients, failed to intercorrelate significantly in 20 of 21 correlations. He concludes:

> It seems clear that the conclusions drawn about the effects of therapy may vary tremendously, depending upon the measures used to define improvements. (Maher, 1966, p. 471)

Traditional psychotherapy has been criticized also along an entirely different dimension: availability. Hollingshead and Redlich (1958) published a now classic study of mental health care delivery in New Haven. Their study yielded three major findings: (1) the rate or prevalence of mental illness, as diagnosed, is significantly related to social class; (2) the types of mental illness are significantly related to social class; and (3) for a given diagnostic type (e.g., neuroses), the form of psychological treatment received by patients is significantly related to their social class.

The implications of these findings in the New Haven study are multiple. Apparently, psychotherapists, as people embedded in their social order, are subject to employing those biases and stereotypes prevalent in the historical moment. Psychotherapists are generally people with middle-class backgrounds and inclinations. Skilled psychotherapists remain in short supply. Psychotherapy remains a service enjoyed disproportionately by the "elite." Psychology can responsively and responsibly contribute to constructive social change only if psychologists as people do not fail to recognize the implications of their own social origins; and only if training and practice change in sensitive conjunction with changing social needs.

Alternatives to Traditional Psychotherapy

Behavior Therapy Variously seen as a challenge to traditional psychotherapy or a different approach to different sorts of problems, behavior therapy addresses itself to overtly manifest behaviors, rather than inner experiences, feelings, fantasies, memories, or personal meanings. Behavior therapy refers to a growing array of techniques based on the psychological principles of learning theory. Advocates of behavior therapy argue that their treatment methods generally take less time and are more easily taught and applied than psychotherapy—hence, less costly and more widely available to the public.

Proponents of behavior therapy do not necessarily dispute that maladaptive responses might have developed as a consequence of childhood, or later, experience, However, they contend that the circumstances of acquisition may not be essential or relevant to the problem of extinction—that is, the elimination of symptomatic behaviors. The following is a capsule sampling of behavior therapy techniques:

1 *Desensitization techniques.* Joseph Wolpe (1958) calls his technique *systematic desensitization,* or *reciprocal inhibition.* It is most effectively used against specific anxiety syndromes, such as a phobia. Essentially, because anxious responses are incompatible with muscular relaxation, Wolpe teaches his patients to relax—a kind of autohypnosis—in the face of anxiety-laden stimuli. First, the therapist and patient generate a hierarchical list of related stimuli in order of increasing anxiety. For example, a patient with a phobia of heights might produce a list with "looking at aerial view photographs" low on the hierarchy, "climbing a hill" farther along the hierarchy, and "looking down over a skyscraper's parapet" at the top of the hierarchy. The patient is trained to relax and then presented with the least disturbing stimulus on his "hierarchy." Increasingly disturbing stimuli are presented until the patient reaches a threshold of anxiety. The stimulus is then quickly removed, and the patient is helped to relax again. Treatment is terminated when the patient has established relaxation as a response in the presence of the most severely anxiety-laden stimuli on his original list. In one well-known case, a young boy severely phobic of cats began treatment by learning to look at the word "cat," then pictures of cats, while maintaining relaxation. Eventually a cat was brought into the room in a cage, and moved closer by increments. Ultimately, the boy and the cat were eating out of the same dish.

2 *Operant conditioning.* By the timely control of *reinforcements,* desired behaviors may be learned or relearned, and undesired behaviors may be unlearned. These techniques have been employed effectively in the hospital treatment of serious psychological disorders. Such "behavior modification" within an institutional setting simply uses systematic reward of patients for socially acceptable behavior and nonreward of unacceptable behavior. This approach is often useful for patients whose behavior is badly deteriorated; for example, those who need to be resocialized to feed or clothe themselves, or to stop hoarding towels or soiling themselves. (See, for further illustrations, the case studies in the first section of Ullman and Krasner, 1965.)

Often, this technique is implemented for several institutionalized patients at the same time by the setting up of a *token economy.* In such a system, patients are rewarded with tokens every time a staff member sees them engaging in behavior previously designated as worthy of reward (e.g., arriving at the right time and place for meals, or engaging in conversation). Tokens can then be exchanged by patients for desired items at the hospital commissary. Token economies have been tried on a large scale and with apparent success on chronic wards of several large hospitals and at residential schools for severely retarded children.

Clearly, one distinct advantage of such behavioral techniques is that they are easily trainable for paraprofessional mental health workers, and thus applicable economically on a wide scale. Further, a mental hospital aide, nurse, or other staff member participating in such a systematic program is likely to be a more attentive and sensitive observer of each patient—which, potentially, could yield other profoundly significant, if more indirect, gains.

3 *Aversive conditioning.* The underlying principle of aversive conditioning is that the punishment of some preliminary behavior in an undesirable behavior sequence will cause the individual to associate that behavior with anxiety. Because the behavior sequence becomes a *conditioned* stimulus for anxiety, the person will terminate that behavior sequence to avoid the punishment. This technique has been employed with some success in the treatment of transvestites and homosexuals. For example, a homosexual male who seeks such therapy is shown photographs of nude males, and when pupil dilation in his eyes indicates his attraction to the picture he is administered a painful electric shock. After repeated applications of this procedure, the patient has learned to reduce his anxiety over punishment by not responding with pleasure to the photograph.

4 *Training in assertive behavior.* The patient who is having difficulty asserting himself when necessary is trained to stand up for himself by a procedure of role modeling and practice. For example, a patient may "rehearse" a job interview, with the behavior therapist playing the interviewer's role. Through encouragement, feedback, and actual modelling, the therapist trains the patient in the desired behavior.

Critics of behavior therapy techniques suggest that the treatment of isolated target symptoms is superficial; that, with deeper underlying problems, the removal of one symptom may lead to its substitution by another symptom. But, for many behavioral complaints, there is impressive evidence to the contrary (see Ullman and Krasner, 1965, pp. 13-15). Another criticism of behavior therapy is that the therapist's relationship to his patient can be very mechanical and manipulative. As in the illustrative case of the treatment of homosexuality, a determined effort at behavioral *control* is undertaken in learning therapies. Therefore, it is essential to properly conducted behavior therapy that, so far as possible, the patient voluntarily consent to the clinical procedures, after they are explained to him, for the relief of personal conditions he chooses to alleviate. Proponents of behavior therapy would argue that a relatively brief and effective clinical procedure that relieves a source of suffering for the patient does speak for itself. Some psychotherapists have found that they can effectively combine behavior therapy techniques with a more traditional therapeutic relationship involving empathic understanding.

Radical Therapy and Antipsychiatry Quite another critical voice is represented by such men as Thomas Szasz (1970) and R. D. Laing (1961, 1965, 1972). Szasz has written about what he calls "the myth of mental illness." His argument is not so much with the practice of psychotherapy, as with the psychiatric practice of diagnostically classifying people as "insane." He questions the factual basis of such labels and suggests that the diagnostic labeling of a patient is a political act, with legal implications affecting the civil rights of the patient—particularly when hospitalization is involved. Szasz admonishes psychiatrists and psychologists to think carefully about the ethical implications of their powerful decisions; to recognize where their obligations are owed (to patient, relatives, hospital, professional group, employer, military, etc.); and to come out from hiding behind their guise of elevated authority and face the real moral conflicts inherent in human relations between equals in a psychotherapeutic endeavor.

Laing has pioneered, and with feisty eloquence, a recognition of the essential resourcefulness in a flight to psychosis and the essential insanity of our social order. He has advocated the removal of arbitrary and artificial barriers between doctor and patient, and established therapeutic communities like Kingsley Hall where staff and patients live together. Hence, in such rehabilitative settings psychological transformations parallel social transformations where doctor and patient alike are encouraged to "discover the wholeness of being human." Drawing from his clinical practice in London, his psychoanalytic background, and his inventive community treatment of "mad" patients, Laing has generated insights about human relationships and international relationships in a mad world sorely in need of social transformations. Examining the barrier society erects between "sanity" and "madness," Laing questions the soundness of society. A case in point: a girl of seventeen says she's terrified that the atom bomb is inside her. This is a delusion. We place her in a mental hospital. A man says he has his finger on a button that can blow up the yellow race. We make him a general of our armies. Laing concludes, "The statesmen of the world who boast and threaten that they have Doomsday weapons are far more dangerous, and far more estranged from 'reality' than many of the people on whom the label 'psychotic' is affixed" (1965, p. 12).

In a speech delivered in 1968 to the London Conference on the Dialectics of Liberation, Laing applied his clinical insights into the psychology of madness to chillingly illuminate the bizarre involvement of the United States in a war in Indochina. He titled his speech "The Obvious," because

> . . . the obvious can be dangerous. The deluded man frequently finds his delusions so obvious that he can hardly credit the good faith of those who do not share them. Hitler regarded it as perfectly obvious that the Jews were a poison to the Aryan race and hence required extermination. What is obvious to Lyndon Johnson is not at all obvious to Ho Chi Minh. (1972, p. 110)

Thus, Laing attempts to psychologically diagnose a social reality. He examines the Vietnam war in terms of the psychological mechanisms of delusion, depersonalization, and paranoid projection. He likens political propaganda to the "mystifying" communications in families that induce psychoses in individuals, and suggests the existence of "collective paranoid projective systems that operate on large scales." In Laing's terms:

> We attribute to Them exactly what We are doing to Them. Because We are seeing ourselves in Them, but we do not know that we are. We think that They are Them, but They are actually Us. (Laing, 1972, p. 124)

And Laing argues that when a president exhorts his combat commanders to "Come home with that coonskin on the wall," one may recognize "the most primitive analogical 'thinking', behind which lies a hinterland of fantasy one hardly dares contemplate" (1972, p. 120).

Beyond the writings and lecturing of such men as R. D. Laing, the radical therapy movement has sought to exert, through the practice of psychotherapy, a deliberate influence upon social change. Radical therapists subscribe to a treatment orientation that stresses "consciousness raising" above "adaptation." The practice of radical therapy has become associated with such social movements as Women's Liberation and Gay Liberation, as well as with the treatment of other chronically oppressed or misunderstood groups. The radical therapist focuses his attention on helping an oppressed person find his anger and locate appropriate action to eliminate oppressive conditions in his environment.

PSYCHOHISTORY

An exploration of the psychology of individuals and its relationship to social change cannot be complete without considering the important contributions of Erik H. Erikson (1950, 1969). His wise and sophisticated teaching and writings have created a new field of study: psychobiography and psychohistory.

Erikson's work belongs to a broad tradition of "culture and personality" study that originated with Freud's efforts to understand primitive and basic foundations of culture as derivatives of the infantile elements of individual personality (see Chapter 5). The field of culture and personality studies has included the important work of such people as Clyde Kluckhohn (1951) and Florence Kluckhohn (1967), Ruth Benedict (1938), and John Whiting and Irvin Child (1953). A related field of study has utilized empirical measurement of individual personality variables to describe "national character" or predict social change. Examples of this are the illumination of the "authoritarian personality" (Adorno et al., 1950) and McClelland and Winter's (1969) research on the "achievement motive" and its relationship to entrepreneurial activity and economic development (see Chapter 3).

Erikson's personality theory extends the basic psychoanalytic model of *psychosexual* development to take into account the *psychosocial* interplay of the individual and his social environment. His essential method is the psychoanalytic approach to insight. As Erikson has stated, "I have nothing to offer except a way of looking at things" (1950, p. 403). His manner of looking at things—whether this be growth and play in a child, child rearing among the Sioux, or the childhood development of Gandhi—is best described by Erikson's phrase for Gandhi's technique of social intervention: "engagement at close range" (1969, p. 434).

Erikson has warned:

> To reconcile historical and psychological methodologies, we must first learn to deal jointly with the fact that psychologies and psychologists are subject to historical laws and that historians and historical records are subject to those of psychology. Having learned in clinical work that the individual is apt to develop an amnesia concerning his most formative experiences in childhood, we are also forced to recognize a universal blind spot in the makers and interpreters of history: they ignore the fateful function of childhood in the fabric of society. Historians and philosophers recognize a "female principle" in the world, but not the fact that man is born and reared by women. They debate principles of formal education, but neglect the fateful dawn of individual consciousness. They forever insist on a mirage of progress which promises that man's (the male's) logic will lead to reason, order, and peace, while each step toward this mirage brings new hostile alignments which lead to war, and worse. Moralistic man and rationalizing man continues to identify himself with abstractions of himself, but refuses to see how he became what he really is and how, as an emotional and political

being, he undoes with infantile compulsions and impulsions what his thought has invented and what his hands have built. All of this has its psychological basis—namely, the individual's unconscious determination never to meet his childhood anxiety face to face again, and his superstitious apprehension lest a glance at the infantile origins of his thought and schemes may destroy his single-minded stamina. He therefore prefers enlightenment away from himself; which is why the best minds have often been least aware of themselves. . . .

Every adult, whether he is a follower or a leader, a member of a mass or of an elite, was once a child. He was once small. A sense of smallness forms a substratum in his mind, ineradicably. His triumphs will be measured against this smallness, his defeats will substantiate it. The questions as to who is bigger and who can do or not do this or that, and to whom—these questions fill the adult's inner life far beyond the necessities and the desirabilities which he understands and for which he plans. (Erikson, 1950, pp. 403ff.)

Erikson points out that there is no universal cure for the fact that "each generation must develop out of its childhood," accompanied by a residue of infantile fears. Psychoanalysts attempt to alleviate this in individual cases. But it is incumbent upon each generation to overcome its own particular brand of childhood, and to develop a new brand of childhood, with its own promises and pitfalls. And, Erikson adds this further sobering observation:

. . . the fact remains that the human being in early childhood learns to consider one or the other aspect of bodily function as evil, shameful, or unsafe. There is no culture which does not use a combination of these devils to develop, by way of counterpoint, its own style of faith, pride, certainty, and initiative. (Erikson, 1950, p. 406)

Hence, since man's first acquaintance with reality comes through a painful testing of "inner and outer goodnesses and badnesses," he remains ready to anticipate from the world around him "that which, in fact, endangers him from within." Here, Erikson is speaking of man's proclivity to project his own angry drives, his own feelings of humiliation and smallness, onto an image of the *obvious* "enemy," as Laing has also indicated. Thus, man's fears of catastrophic events, foes, invasions, encirclements, and shameful belittlement characterize not only his personal affairs but also the shadow-show of world affairs.

Erikson (1950, pp. 408-11) has gone so far as to catalogue a set of universal anxieties to which all men (and women) are subject during their development, and to which people refer as they construct the meaning of their social actuality. These anxieties involve:

1. Suddenness and sudden loss
2. Manipulation
3. Interruption
4. Impoverishment, both nutritional and sensual
5. Loss of autonomy, and being closed up
6. Restraint, but also loss of outer bounds
7. Attack from the rear
8. Exposure, and falling
9. Castration, and remaining small
10. Immobilization, but also lack of guidance
11. Being left, and (especially for females) being left empty
12. Being raped

Erikson suggests that man's ultimate sense of humanity, identity, and integrity depends upon the interaction of his major childhood crises, his experience of "social health," and the solidarity of his culture. Erikson further indicates the emergence of those transcendent individuals whose efforts to attain a personal equilibrium carry them beyond their cultural origins and lead them to implicate their entire social group in identity crises and change, for better or for worse. Erikson has thus illuminated Hitler's rise to power in a ready Germany, as well as Gandhi's mobilization of militant nonviolence in India. Such psychohistorical studies help us to understand the convergence of a historical moment and a strong individual who shapes the lives of others as he bridges a personal crossroads.

Erikson tasks psychologists to combine their insight with responsibility for the ways in which childhood anxiety is produced and exploited in the form of "collective panics" and "afflictions of the collective mind." He emphasizes that his catalogue of anxieties "could be taken out of their context of childhood and serve as headings for a treatise on group panics and their propagandistic exploitation." And he adds this exhortation:

> This then is one of our jobs: to perfect methods which, in given situations, facilitate the elucidation of such prejudices, apprehensions, and lapses of judgment as emanate from infantile rage and from the adult's defenses against his latent infantile anxiety. (Erikson, 1950, p. 413)

And Erikson enjoins us not to seek facile solutions from psychology. He insists that if clinical experience has yielded us some capacity to detect meaningful connections in the relationship between childhood anxieties and social upheavals, we still do not possess the insight or power to "synthesize" or "manufacture" desirable personality types, to prescribe the "right" timing or dosage of child-rearing ingredients, or to "answer" the questions implicit in societal needs. Erikson does not believe that "mere scientific synthesis" could construct "a foolproof system which would lead our children in a desired direction and avoid an undesirable one." He anticipates the regrettable potential of psychology to become a new system of "scientific" superstitions since, as he observes, "when men concentrate on an uncharted area of human existence, they aggrandize this area to become the universe, and they reify its center as the prime reality" (1950, p. 419). Such schemes reduce men to "nothing but their facsimiles," a model more conducive to exploitation and manipulation, but not the basis for an essentially human psychology.

Rather, Erikson reaffirms the essential values he sees in the psychoanalytic method of cure-research: observation and self-observation; objectivity and participation; knowledge and imagination; tolerance and indignation. In such a "judicious partnership," Erikson suggests, both analyst and patient find "the capacity for creative change in further partnerships." But Erikson also recognizes that, beyond the dyadic partnership of psychoanalysis, psychologists must provide models of judicious collaboration on a larger scale. As he writes:

> The alternative to an exploitation of the lowest common denominator of men is the deliberate appeal to their latent intelligence, and the systematic cultivation of new forms of group discussion. (Erikson, 1950, p. 420)

And Erickson further asserts:

I fully believe that the new techniques of discussion which are now being developed—and this in industry as well as in education—have a good chance of replacing the reassurance which once emanated from a continuity of tradition. (Erikson, 1950, p. 421)

Chapter 3 of this volume is devoted to an examination of "these new forms of group discussion."

Chapter 3

Psychology and Change in Groups

In most American cities (particularly along the East and West coasts), it is likely that a person could participate in some sort of "group encounter" during any weekend. Newspapers carry classified ads such as:

> Weekend of Encounter
> for single adults concerned
> about how to meet people.
> Call Institute for Human
> Improvement.

or

> Gestalt Couples Workshop
> Friday thru Sunday
> Center for Growth and Awareness

The proliferation of group experiences in recent years, and the saturation coverage groups have received in magazines (from *Time* to

Psychology Today), television, books, movies (witness *Bob and Carol and Ted and Alice*), as well as institutes, universities, etc., has led many observers to consider the spread of groups a major social movement.

Indeed, the rapid diffusion of this social innovation is reflected in the plethora of names that supposedly refer to variations on the basic group program. To name a partial list, there are encounter groups, T-groups, self-analytic groups, human relations groups, couples groups, sensory awareness groups, therapy groups, marathon groups, organizational effectiveness groups, gestalt groups, and motivational groups. Groups have been employed to facilitate change or growth in industry, education, medical and psychiatric training, community relations, religious seminaries, Peace Corps training, penitentiaries, drop-in centers, and even in the U.S. State Department.

Significantly, psychological group work has attracted over the last decade some of the nation's most eminent psychologists and infiltrated several of the major institutions of education, professional training, and treatment. It has also provided the technical and inspirational foundation for the hundred or so "new wave," experimental, and nonestablishmentarian growth centers that have been operating across the country since Esalen established the vogue in California. Just as significantly, the group movement has attracted the fly-by-night, the "snake oil" salesman, the self-styled guru, and the half-trained enthusiast into the ranks of group leaders. Already the growing literature on groups has attained substantial proportions, although proportionately few truly sophisticated *theoretical* works have arisen specifically out of the group field. In our view, the major theoretical works remain those of Freud (1951), Bion (1961), Bennis and Shepard (1956), Slater (1966), and Bales (1970), although important phenomenological works (e.g., Rogers, 1967), technical books (e.g., Yalom, 1970; Whitaker and Lieberman, 1964), and many empirical studies are available.

WHAT ARE PSYCHOLOGICAL GROUPS?

Considering the vast heterogeneity of group offerings in various social contexts, it may be asked what constitutes a basis for classifying the multitude of group experiences as related phenomena belonging together or inviting comparison. After all, men have always formed groups, on hillsides, around campfires, in bunkers, on committees, or teams and in spontaneous social action. Actually, there are common elements in small psychological groups that deserve note and will help our further discussion of change in groups.

At this point we will outline a general model of process and evolution in psychological groups. Later, we will examine the contributions of spokesmen for various specific types of groups so that the reader can derive a more elaborated sense of the commonalities and the distinctions in the conglomerate field of group work. All this is essential preparation for the heart of this chapter: an extensive, illustrative case account of the progress of two particular individuals through one adolescent human relations group.

A "Bare-Bones" General Model of Groups

Most groups (with the exception of open-ended therapy groups) have certain structural similarities: a finite membership (generally eight to eighteen members), and a finite time duration (a weekend, "semester," year). Usually there is a leader—although a recent development has been leaderless groups such as the consciousness-raising groups in the Women's Liberation Movement, or encounter groups held in the presence of a tape-recorded set of instructions. However, ordinarily a leader, or coleader team, calls the group together, recruits members, and undertakes a primary responsibility to facilitate the expression of thoughts and feelings by group members, to protect individuals from psychological "overexposure," and commonly to provide some form of cognitive input through orientation, observations, interpretations, or perhaps even minilectures.

The first issue faced by any group is one of *trust,* in all its ramifications. According to Jack R. Gibb (1970), trust is the base from which all other group developments emerge. One aspect of this issue is the question of the group's boundaries: who is, or is not, a member? Who else learns about what is said here? What are the rules governing confidentiality? Who intends to continue to be a member, and who will drop out? Throughout the life of a group, trust remains the linchpin of all activity: trust that the leader is competent; trust that the group is safe; trust that other group members are listening; trust that self-expression is constructive; trust that risks are tolerable; trust that change is desirable and possible; trust that others also care about the experience being shared.

Another issue that is important from the beginning for group members is *the conditions of belonging:* what is asked of a member of this group? How will each individual be accepted? What must be personally sacrificed for the benefit of the group? What rules must be followed, and by whose authority? What can each member hope to gain from belonging to this group?

The reciprocal issue to that of *belonging* is the nature of personal *autonomy* within the group: what is the balance between the demands for conformity and the recognition of individuality in this group? Are differences acknowledged and respected? Hence, at a relatively early stage in the life of a group, each member begins to become aware of himself in relationship to other, quite separate, people. Generally, it is this emergent awareness that generates the true beginnings of group interaction. The nature of that interaction follows from the nature of each member's awareness of himself in relationship to others, and, of course, from the specific goals and membership of each group. For example, two individuals may discover that they hold passionate loyalties to opposite sides of a political issue, and a confrontation ensues. Or, discussion may begin when one group member expresses his awareness of another in a stereotyped way, such as "jock," or "chick," or "conservative," or "intellectual." One member may realize that he fears or envies something about another. The unfolding of group interaction surrounding such issues constitutes the basis for *shared experience* in the group.

Out of such discussions follows some reconsideration of how to relate to one another. Initial naïve expectations about the group, about self and others, are gradually discarded, old forms of authority are questioned (or defied), and group members commit themselves to a state of *interdependence.* At this stage in the group, people are listening more carefully to one another, and offering *feedback* to others (e.g., "This is how you sound to me. . . ."). Group members struggle to overcome their resistance to admitting to themselves how much of their previous manner of relating to others has been what might be variously called defensive façade, or rigid dogma, or unresponsive role playing. In a supportive atmosphere, individuals undertake personal responsibility for the results of what they say or do to others. With the insight gained from mutual listening and responsive feedback, group members confront the challenges of change. Previously unseen alternatives become new possibilities, whether for individual behavior, organizational policy, or group conflict resolution. Indeed, the essential learning in such group experiences is learning how to continue learning; the essential change is in the participants' ability to change.

Generally, it is in the midst of such learning that most groups encounter their own ending. There is a terminal period in which members celebrate their attachments and grieve together their immanent losses. The final task for group members is one of *integrating* and *internalizing* the benefits of their group experience so that each person may carry from the group the means for further growth and learning.

A Brief History of Groups

The initial and generic form of a small group program, the T-group,[1] originated serendipitously when a psychologist was asked to assist in the engineering of constructive social change. The year was 1946, a new Fair Employment Practices Act had been passed in Connecticut along with an implementing agency, the Connecticut Interracial Commission, and psychologist Kurt Lewin was asked to help train community leaders to cope more effectively with intergroup tensions. Lewin was director of a fledgling Research Center for Group Dynamics at the Massachusetts Institute of Technology, and he organized a workshop in New Britain, Connecticut for businessmen, labor leaders, and educators. Lewin did not intend a T-group format, but rather a workshop for training in conflict resolution and social attitude change. Three groups of ten members each were led by Leland Bradford, Kenneth Benne, and Ronald Lippitt. Lewin led a staff of social psychologists whose purpose was to monitor and research the process and outcome of these conference groups. Hence, the laboratory aspect of the groups, the analysis of group dynamics, was considered distinct from the actual group process, and feedback was not built into the program. Workshop meetings consisted of discussions of community problems, as well as some role playing.

---

[1] The "T" stands for "training" as in "sensitivity training group," "human relations training group," or "leadership training group." The rapid growth in popularity of groups is evident to one of the authors who is nearly embarrassed to be offering a definition of a T-group that must be unnecessary for most readers of this volume, but who telephoned the Harvard Graduate School of Education six years ago to ask for the name of the coordinator of their T-group program and was told "I'm sorry, we don't serve tea in the afternoons during the summer."

In the evenings following the small group sessions, the leaders got together with the team of researchers to pool their observations and coded ratings of group process. Some group members quickly learned about these evening staff briefings, and a few asked to be included. Lewin agreed, and despite the reservations of his staff about exposing their own responses to the group participants and, reciprocally, exposing the group participants to their candid observations, the impromptu arrangement proved exciting for both staff and participants. Eventually, all program participants attended these evening sessions, and they began to respond to the staff's observations and interpretations, often extending these meetings for hours of self-analytic interaction. It soon became apparent that the New Britain project had stumbled upon a vital new format for individuals to participate in groups and concurrently observe their own behavior. In short, through interaction, observation, and confrontation, group members could learn an immense amount about themselves, and other people, and the ways in which individuals related in groups.

Inspired by the potentials of this new educational technique, Bradford, Lippit, and Benne (Lewin died only a few months after that seminal program in New Britain) organized a similar three-week laboratory group program on a wider scale the following summer in Bethel, Maine. During subsequent summer programs, the group technique evolved until feedback became an integral feature of group sessions, not a separate matter of postsession evening quarterbacking. From these origins, the National Training Laboratory in Bethel, Maine was established as an ongoing operation within the National Education Association. Today there are hundreds of NTL-trained group leaders, and thousands of annual participants sent to Bethel, or to NTL-sponsored groups, by school systems, universities, government agencies, industries, professional groups, etc. The essential elements of such NTL programs have been (1) the opportunity to learn more about self or organization through an ongoing group experience; (2) the opportunity, quoting Robert Burns out of context, "to see ourselves as others see us"; and (3) the opportunity, in a safe environment, to consider the possibilities of change. Over the years since 1950, NTL groups have grown more individual-oriented, placing ever greater emphasis upon interpersonal interaction, honest self-expression, candid personal feedback, and *personal* change.

Paralleling the evolution of NTL, T-groups came into use as a psychological laboratory at universities. In addition to the Center for Group Dynamics at MIT, several of Lewin's students constituted an Institute for the Study of Group Dynamics at the University of Michigan. And, Robert F. Bales headed the Laboratory of Social Relations at Harvard University, out of which emerged the first self-analytic group course at a university (now called Social Relations 1200) and a huge yield of theory and research by such men as Bales (1970), Slater (1966), Mills (1964), and Mann (1967).

Another, and somewhat variant, development in the evolution of intensive group experiences is described by Carl Rogers (1970). He and his associates at the Counseling Center of the University of Chicago were asked by the Veterans Administration in 1946 to construct a "brief but intensive course of training" for personal counselors to help them work more effectively with post-World War II GIs. Rogers' staff decided to blend experiential and cognitive learning in an intensive group in which trainees met for several hours each day. Group interaction focused on each trainee's acquiring a better understanding of himself, especially aspects of personal style or attitude that seemed self-defeating in a counseling relationship. Rogers emphasizes that the Chicago group's stress on "therapeutic value for the individual," on personal growth and interpersonal relationships, distinguishes his work as a thrust in the group movement separate from the human relations skills orientation of T-groups at NTL. Rogers' eventual pioneer work with encounter groups can be seen as a direct development from his group work in Chicago within the framework of client-centered therapy (see Chapter 2).

Group therapy, originating from a traditional medical model of the treatment of illness and relief of suffering, has had its own development separate from that of T-groups, laboratory groups, and encounter groups. J. L. Moreno (1953) first used the term group therapy. He is most distinctly associated with the creation of specialized group techniques of psychodrama, but he reports that prior to 1920 he was running the first bona fide psychotherapy groups—with prostitutes. As early as 1905, Joseph Hershey Pratt, an internist, ran groups for tubercular patients that exploited a group's cohesiveness and supportiveness, and personal testimonials to help alleviate the sense of depression and isolation that Pratt recognized was a psychological irritant of the physical disease.

Psychoanalytic mavericks, like Alfred Adler, explored group techniques out of their conviction of the social causes of human conflict. As psychoanalytic psychiatry moved more in the directions of ego psychology and interpersonal theory, a more receptive climate toward groups developed among clinicians.

In analyzing any social movement, it seems always "up for grabs" whether the principal germinative factors are principle or principal, that is, ideological or economic. Suffice it to say that the post-World War II crunch of veterans in need of psychiatric help, and the relative scarcity of available professionals, urged and necessitated a vastly accelerated adoption of group therapeutic techniques. The economic pressures on the adequate delivery of health care remains today a strong argument for even wider use of group formats for psychotherapy.

The major prongs of development in the group movement have already been described. The variations that have proliferated over the past decade or so are evolutions of some form of T-group, encounter group, or therapy group according to particular theories of human nature, or in response to particular needs.

Alternative Models of Groups

In view of the multidimensional history of groups, our bare-bones model of groups might well be qualified to take into account the particular frameworks of various spokesmen for T-groups, encounter groups, and therapy groups. Therefore, at this juncture some other representative views of groups merit our attention. Hopefully, the following discussion of T-groups and encounter groups will give the reader some impression of the distinct variations in "flavor" that exist in the broad field of psychological group work.

T-groups

One of the cognitive aids often used in T-groups has been the Jo-Hari Window (Luft, 1963), which can serve us as a cognitive aid at the moment to help summarize the goals and the work of T-groups (particularly the kind conducted for organizations). The sketch that follows presents the basic elements of the Jo-Hari Window.

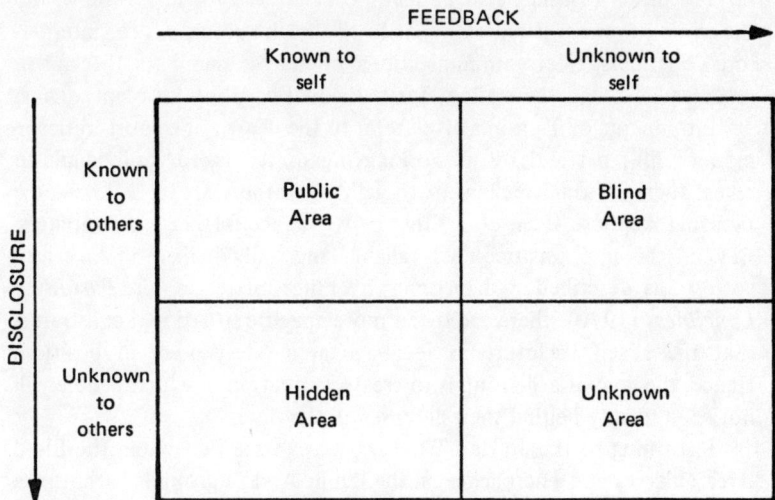

From *Group Processes: An Introduction to Group Dynamics* by Joseph Luft, by permission of National Press Books.

Figure 3-1

What has been depicted in the Window is a diagram of a person's life situation in terms of who knows what about him. A few illustrative cases would provide the best explanations of the scheme. For example, a person is aware of feeling extremely tense upon entering a group, but attempts to begin interacting with others while maintaining a cool demeanor. This secret anxiety lies in the Hidden Area. Another group member incessantly talks, interrupting others and droning on unaware of the irritation, frustration, and boredom felt by other group members. He is blind to a personal style which offends others.

T-groups focus upon expanding the Public Area. In other words, they try to enlarge the range of an individual's self-awareness as well as the range of what others can know about him. Two basic group processes accomplish the goal of expanding the Public Area. Through feedback, the individual receives from others valuable data about how he is perceived. This helps diminish his Blind Area. Or, through disclosure, the individual can reveal more of himself to others, thus reducing his Hidden Area. Clearly, the two processes may be reciprocal, since group members more readily offer feedback to a group member who has given of himself.

The intent behind a schematization such as the Jo-Hari Window, and the group processes it represents, is to clarify the potentials for interpersonal openness, freer communications among the members of teams or organizations, and the options for individual or group problem solving.

Proponents of T-groups often refer to the dearth of opportunities in modern life, particularly in working organizations, for individuals to reveal their personal feelings or thoughts to others, or to receive some personal response from others that may enhance further self-awareness. Beyond the emphasis upon self-reliance and individualism in American society, as described with urgency by Philip Slater in *The Pursuit of Loneliness* (1970), there are often more specific situational constraints that make self-disclosure or feedback an anxiety-laden proposition. Hence, the goal of a T-group is to create a situation in which people will not need to stay behind their defenses all the time.

Returning to the Jo-Hari Window, we can see that when the Blind Area enlarges and encroaches on the Public Area, a group is harboring a lot of unfinished business, or hidden agendas. These are dependency, fight, flight, and pairing—dimensions originally conceptualized by W. R. Bion (he called them "basic assumptions") in his landmark essay *Experiences in Groups* (1961). Dependency, fight, flight, and pairing are implicit group strategies for responding to stressful unfinished business; but they are essentially defensive postures that interfere with the work of confrontation, disclosure, and feedback, which would produce learning, change, and growth. Much of the T-group leader's interpretive work is an effort to illuminate for the group its tacit emotional consensus to block work through the defenses of dependency upon authority, passivity and lethargy, protestations of helplessness, retreat or withdrawal, conflict-avoidance, apathy, complaint, attack, coalitions, collusions and cliques, or manipulative alliances. As such obstacles to group work are reduced the group members become more capable of attending realistically to their unfinished business, and there is more general sharing of the Public Area indicated in the Jo-Hari Window, in which a group member is increasingly aware of both himself and others.

Warren Bennis (1962) has summarized the goals of T-group, or laboratory training, as (1) self-insight or self-knowledge; (2) understanding of the obstacles to effective group functioning; (3) understanding of interpersonal transactions in groups; and (4) developing skills for diagnosing the behavior of people, groups, and organizations.

Bennis emphasizes that change is "the participant's privilege, but choice is something trainers must emphasize." Hence, the T-group leader does not seek to change group members in any particular ways. Rather, what he seeks to change is the members' awareness of choices, the costs of alternatives, and their ability to change in accordance with their own choices. The means employed by the group leader is the creation of an atmosphere of inquiry, authentic communication, and collaboration.

Bennis and Shepard (1956) have written "A Theory of Group Development," which explicates the group processes over time that accomplish the "meta-goals" of laboratory training, and remove the barriers to group work and interpersonal communication. Bennis and Shepard derive their theory from Bion's model of basic assumptions among group members, the defensive modalities for responding to the unfinished business we mentioned earlier. These authors consider the principal obstacles to valid interpersonal communication (i.e., a working group) to lie in group members' rigidities of perception and response that are the residue of anxious experiences with "particular love or power figures," and are carried over into new situations in which they are inappropriate. In Bion's terms, this proclivity of an individual member to impose the precipitates of his past as his basis for interpreting the present, is his "valence" for a particular defensive modality, or basic assumption in the group.

Bennis and Shepard identify five group personality types, which seem roughly analogous to the individual valence tendencies postulated by Bion. These types are (1) "dependent" individuals who seek direction or nurturance (Bion's valence for dependency); (2) "counterdependent" individuals who deny or avoid dependency concerns, or who express dependent hostility in the form of complaints (Bion's "fight-flight" valence); (3) "overpersonal" individuals who seek excessive or unrealistic degrees of intimacy and avoid expression of aggression (Bion's valence for pairing); and (4) "counter-personal" individuals who deny or reject intimacy needs (again, Bion's "fight-flight" valence). The fifth personality type is the "independent" individual who is relatively unconflicted in areas of either *authority* or *intimacy*, or both; and who is thus less susceptible to the extreme emotional vicissitudes of the group, and better able to perceive and cope realistically with events at critical stages of the group's life cycle. Bennis and Shepard recognize two basic phases of group activity, "dependence" and "interdependence," each divided into three substages. During the dependence phase the central issue in the group is relations with authority and the distribution of *power;* during the second phase, interdependence, the central issue is relations with one another and the distribution of *affection.* Bennis and Shepard quote Freud's observation that "each member is bound by libidinal ties on one hand to the leader ... and on the other hand to the other members of the group." Dynamically, Bennis and Shepard represent the developmental model of group members first coping with their unrealistic expectations or distorted perceptions of the leader, then addressing themselves to the emotional aspects of intimate relationship with one another.

The stages of group development in Bennis and Shepard's model progress in the following sequence:

Phase I: Dependence

Subphase 1. Dependence-Flight: "The first days of group life are filled with behavior whose remote, as well as immediate, aim is to ward off anxiety." Members seek security through introduction rituals, group goal seeking, and attempts at structure, but maintain interaction at a relatively shallow level. They avoid acknowledgment and confrontation of dependency themes, particularly in relations with the group leader. Although unspoken, anxiety is evident. During this subphase, dependent personality types dominate the group.

Subphase 2. Counterdependence-Fight: Increasing disenchantment with the leader, who has not rescued them from their initial anxiety, divides members into "warring subgroups." One subgroup attempts to offer the entire group the structure (e.g., elected member leaders, meeting agendas, a "constitution"), which the leader has refused to provide; the other subgroup, displacing its hostility to the member-surrogates who would take his place, resists all such efforts to contribute structure. Throughout the group, members feel generally angry and helpless. The leader is alternately bullied and ignored, and attacks upon him become increasingly open and direct. Overt hostility is great; Bennis and Shepard consider this subphase "the most stressful and unpleasant in the life of the group." Conflicted dependent and counterdependent personality types dominate group process.

Subphase 3. Resolution-Catharsis: The crescendo of disenchantment in subphase 2 has reached a pass at which the group is threatened by splintering into irreconcilable subgroups, and extinction. But, as Bennis and Shepard explain, along with the degenerative chain of events through subphases 1 and 2, "there has been a simultaneous, though less obvious, mobilization of constructive forces." Bennis and Shepard continue:

> First, within each of the warring subgroups bonds of mutual support have grown. The group member no longer feels helpless and isolated. Second, the trainer's role, seen as weak or manipulative in the dependence orientation, can also be perceived as permissive. Third, his interpretations, though openly ignored, have been secretly attended to. And, as the second and third points imply, some members of the group are less the prisoners of the dependence-counterdependence dilemma than others. (Bennis & Shepard, 1956, p. 423)

These relatively unconflicted members, the independents, now assume a visible and effective role in the group, serving as catalytic agents to precipitate a "barometric event." That is, the leader is finally challenged directly; he may be symbolically overthrown or "killed" (e.g., asked to leave the room or denied his customary chair). Following this cathartic event the group no longer maintains its intimidating fantasies of the leader's authority, rational analysis replaces "transference emotionality" (i.e., unrealistic expectations and distorted perceptions of the leader), and from this point onward "the problems of submission and domination rarely emerge as significant group issues." The group has achieved autonomy; a new sense of solidarity emerges as the group evolves its own leaders while more realistically accepting the leader as a person fulfilling the role of teacher or therapist. Bennis and Shepard observe the delicacy of subphase 3, and the possibility that no sufficiently unconflicted members will emerge with sufficient strength to catalyze the barometric revolt—a condition that consigns the group to vacillate between subphases 1 and 2 without ever proceeding toward significant intimacy and integration as a group. Generally, however, the revolt constitutes a rapid bridge to phase II, where the group then explores the implications of the mutually shared responsibilities that finally have been accepted.

Phase II: Interdependence

Subphase 4. Enchantment-Flight: Group members attempt to remain unanimous, mutually supportive, and happy in all their activities. Everything is expected to be "sweetness and light." Individual differences among members and opposing opinions are suppressed; latent animosities and rivalries are scrupulously ignored. Eventually, "the solidarity and harmony become more and more illusory" under the pressures of denied aggression, and increased anxiety in the group reflects the scope of latent issues, or unfinished business, that are being inattended. Overpersonal members dominate group process during this subphase.

Subphase 5. Disenchantment-Fight: Growing disenchantment with the prevailing group myth of unqualified solidarity and intimacy again produces conflict between two subgroups: the first composed of overpersonal members who attempt to perpetuate and personify the myth of togetherness; the second subgroup composed of counterpersonal members who angrily resist further interpersonal involvement. These latter subgroup members assert that intimacy is a fraud or a will-o'-the-wisp that inhibits self-actualization; they exalt individualism and contend that familiarity breeds contempt. This subphase is characterized by general disillusionment, apathy, withdrawal, boredom, and perhaps increased absenteeism.

Subphase 6. Consensual Validation: In the face of approaching termination, members feel compelled to confront once again the group's goal definitions and achievements (especially if an objective evaluation of group and member performance is to be made, for example in the form of grades). Initially this process aggravates depression and mutual disparagement as opposing subgroups conduct a post mortem and blame one another for the group's failure. Once again, group members find themselves in the throes of a crisis of confidence (as in subphase 3). And, once again, it is the independents—in this case those "whose self-esteem is not threatened by the prospect of intimacy"—who restore members' confidence in the group. By their own unconflicted expressions of confidence in the group they initiate a new period of personal endorsements. If such a barometric event occurs to propel the group out of crisis, a stage of rational analysis and "life review" ensues in which group members assess and accept what they have learned from the experience, in a spirit of sharing, equality, and interdependence.

Encounter Groups

Carl Rogers (1967) has written on "The Process of the Basic Encounter Group," of which he is a founding father. In his approach to groups Rogers attempts to be "simple and naturalistic." He prefers to describe his group experiences rather than build "high-level abstract theory." He insists that he does not attempt "to make profound interpretations of unconscious motives or of some developing group psyche. You will not find me speaking of group myths, or even of dependence and counterdependence. I am not comfortable with such inferences, correct though they may be. At this stage of our knowledge I wish merely to describe the observable events." Rogers' group process description proceeds, "in roughly sequential order," as follows:

1 *Milling around.* This is an initial period of confusion, tense silences, awkwardness, polite chitchat, and a general lack of continuity. Talk is solipsistic. Group members feel frustrated with the relative absence of directorial guidance from a leader, and ask a lot of questions.

2 *Resistance to personal expression or exploration.* A few group members make brief forays into self-revelation. Generally, such communications are barely reciprocated because most other group members remain apprehensive about revealing *themselves*. Individuals put their best façade forward, and lack sufficient trust in the group to risk the vulnerabilities of their inner self.

3 *Description of past feelings.* In the face of ambivalent feelings about self-disclosure, particularly fears over the imagined risks of exposure, group members begin to express their feelings about situations external to the group—back home or at the office. At first, feelings are described rather than expressed, as if they belong only "there and then" rather than "here and now."

4 *Expression of negative feelings.* Rogers observes that the first "here and now" feelings expressed in groups tend to be negative ones, complaints, or attacks upon another group member or the leader. Rogers recognizes that such initial emotional expressions may reflect a group member's prior expectations or demands upon the leader (a view not incompatible with T-group theories like Bennis and Shepard's).

Rogers speculates that negative feelings appear because group members thereby test the freedom and safety of the group atmosphere, and because positive feelings are more difficult and dangerous to express.

5 *Expression and exploration of personally meaningful material.* After the freedom of the group has been tested, and the expression of negative feelings has not created a catastrophe, group members begin to feel that they *belong* enough to offer some significant revelation. In the emergent climate of trust, one group member after another risks disclosure of some deeper facet of himself, and others begin to respond in ways that may facilitate, or hinder, his further exploration.

6 *The expression of immediate interpersonal feelings in the group.* Somewhat akin to feedback, these responses between group members are often less analytic or diagnostic than T-group feedback, and more of an opening of "feelings experienced in the immediate moment by one member toward another." For example, "I really felt close to you then —I wanted to hug you when you said that."

7 *The development of a healing capacity in the group.* Group members manifest a natural and spontaneous capacity to enter into helping relationships with one another, in which they use their often remarkable intuition and understanding to express their caring and facilitate a therapeutic experience for one another.

8 *Self-acceptance and the beginning of change.* Rogers offers many illustrations to emphasize that change begins to be possible for a person when he acknowledges and accepts himself "with all his strengths and weaknesses." Frequently, a group member admits, to himself or others, a painful truth about himself, and consequently feels more authentic, closer to his feelings, and more open to change.

9 *The cracking of façades.* Group members become increasingly impatient and intolerant toward the defenses that preserve rigid or shallow relationships. In pursuit of a more basic encounter they combine and interweave gentle nudges, warm supports, or relentless demands to help one another remove their accustomed masks. Often such moments in the group may be alternately violent and tender.

10 *The individual receives feedback.* This is essentially the T-group process in which a person receives valuable data to help reduce his Blind Areas.

11 *Confrontation.* Whereas feedback is considered generally to be warmly and positively toned, confrontation is far less mild, and often is decidedly negative. One group member directly "levels" with another, and may indeed seem to be leveling *at* him. Often the ultimate result of such confrontations, generally between two people, is a genuinely and mutually supportive dyad.

12 *The helping relationship outside the group sessions.* and
13 *The basic encounter.* and
14 *The expression of positive feelings and closeness.* Rogers observes that the directness and intensity of relationships among group members frequently extend beyond the group's boundaries of time and space. Group members approach one another, and respond to other members' needs, often lingering at a street corner or staying up through the night. The close and direct contact among people, beyond what Rogers observes in ordinary life, is reminiscent of the I-Thou encounter described by Martin Buber. To this Rogers attributes the most central, intense, and change-producing potency of group experience.

15 *Behavior changes in the group.* Rogers notes changes in the participants of an encounter group within the group itself and afterwards. In the group, a person's gestures change, his voice timbre changes, or he shows new resources of thoughtfulness and helpfulness. After group experiences, persons report feeling more openness and spontaneity; more personal tolerance or empathy; more confidence; more freedom in old relationships; deeper relationships; more clarity of feelings, both loving and hostile; more involvement with others; more satisfaction in daily experiences.

We can see that both Bennis and Shepard's model and Rogers' model have in common a developmental conception of group process that evolves over time. Further, both theories recognize the tendency of group participants to turn toward individuals in power in order to facilitate group beginnings. They both also describe the crucial value of interpersonal response giving, in one form or another, and the centrality of group issues surrounding coming together and achieving a sense of closeness.

What distinguishes Bennis and Shepard from Rogers, and, by example, T-groups in general from encounter groups, is largely a matter of focus. It is not simply the style of Bennis and Shepard's exposition that is more analytical, abstract, and didactic than Rogers'. The manifest goals of such groups as Bennis and Shepard describe, within the NTL tradition, selectively concentrate on the group participant's learning through experience to observe, diagnose, and resolve those obstacles to interpersonal, group, and organizational effectiveness that result from human conflicts over authority and power relationships as well as intimacy and emotional relationships. In contrast, the Rogerian genre of encounter group seeks not so much to illuminate and teach group process skills to be transferred directly by the participant for application in other settings. Rather, the goals of an encounter group, as Rogers' description implies, selectively concentrate on the use of group interaction to facilitate the relaxation of personal defenses, the burgeoning of self-awareness, and the actualization of deeper modes of person-to-person intimacy among specific people. Hence, for Rogers, the transfer of group learnings to other settings in the participant's environment is a more diffuse, noncalculated, incidental, and preconceptual byproduct of his own personal growth.

Research on Groups

As in the case of psychotherapy (see Chapter 2), the value of this special psychological technique has been asserted principally in theoretical statements, such as Bennis and Shepard's or Rogers', or in testimonials from practitioners or participants. Although much research has been conducted with groups, most of the studies have focused on relatively trivial group phenomena, or have lacked the scientific rigor necessary to empirically verify the psychological effects of group participation. Hence, until quite recently, very little solid data existed that might indicate the outcomes of group techniques, the dangers, and the relative merits of the various approaches within this patchwork field. Such *measurements* of group process and group outcomes have been especially needed in the face of allegations that encounter-type groups are as transparently worthless as the Emperor's new clothes—or, even worse, that group experiences involve obscure and clinically unsound procedures that assault personal defenses, induce craziness, and pander to people's atavistic longings for a New Jerusalem. (For one critic's view, see Back, 1972.)

Hopefully, the case study that follows shortly in this chapter will offer the reader relatively direct evidence, which he can evaluate for himself. The research study from which this case was derived (Massar, 1972; Pizer, 1972) will also be presented later. However, to date the most comprehensive and definitive study of groups yet conducted has been reported by Lieberman, Yalom, and Miles (1973). At Stanford University, they studied eighteen groups representing ten different approaches to group technique, including the traditional NTL genre of T-group, Rogerian personal growth groups, transactional analysis groups, gestalt, marathon, Esalen-type sensory awareness, and psychoanalytic orientations. There were even two leaderless groups structured around tapes produced by Bell and Howell. The study filled more than sixty thousand IBM cards with an array of measures of group members before, during, and after their group experience.

Lieberman et al. found that 61 percent of the student participants reported changing in positive ways, particularly in terms of increased understanding of inner feelings and increased sensitivity to others. On the other hand, 9.4 percent of the participants were considered to be "casualties," which means, as Yalom et al. defined the term, that these individuals showed evidence of enduring psychological harm six to eight months after termination of their group. Among these casualties were one psychotic episode and one severe depression with a 40-pound weight loss. And, one of the least accurate predictors of a potential casualty was the group leaders' ratings! (The most accurate rating was the judgment of peers in the group.) Based on their interviews and their quantitative data, Lieberman et al. conclude that group learners and group casualties are based on preexisting personality types interacting with specific leadership styles and group climates.

By far the most intriguing aspect of this massive study is the typology of various leadership styles that Lieberman et al. found to be associated with positive and negative outcomes for group members. The similarities and differences in the approaches of group leaders were *not* related to school of thought. Rather, it was the personality style of each group leader that typed his approach to change. Hence, this study does not support the notion that leaders labeled similarly (e.g., T-group or gestalt) actually behave similarly in their groups.

Lieberman et al. identified one type of group leader, the "Energizer," who is characteristically an emotional stimulator, a "true believer" and proselytizer, and the most charismatic in the eyes of group members. Such leaders convey an air of the "turn-on" and a zealousness flavored with religiosity. According to the study, such leaders contributed to the highest rate of casualties among group members, probably because their style of aggressive stimulation created a group climate in which strong attack or rejection occurred. Strikingly, these high-risk leaders did not provide the highest rate of learning. The leaders who were found to contribute to the most learning among their group members have been typed by Lieberman et al. as the "Providers." These group leaders employed only a moderate amount of emotional stimulation and control. But they specialized in a high degree of caring and "meaning attribution" (that is, commenting in ways to help group members make sense of their experience). The researchers call leaders of this type "good daddies." Fifty-eight percent of the participants in their groups manifested noticeable change in the study, while only one of their thirty-six collective members ultimately registered as a casualty. Lieberman et al. describe four other leader types that we will not discuss here. However, the conclusion we do wish to emphasize is that high risk is not necessary for the achievement of maximum growth in a group, and overstimulation by the group leader is a prime expressway toward casualties. Hence, the mass media caricatures of group turn-ons, heady enthusiasm, and brutal confrontation simply do not reflect ingredients related to positive change in group members. Hamlet's disclaimer, "I must be cruel only to be kind," will not work for group leaders. Rather, it is affection, support, and meaningful understanding that seem to maximize growth and minimize risk. The distinctions clarified by this carefully wrought study mark a new step toward the rigorous examination of an important and controversial psychological technique for promoting change.

Critics of Groups as Instruments of Social Change

The humane goals of groups that facilitate growth and self-actualization for individuals or organizations have come under attack from various, and quite diverse, quarters both within and outside the psychological community. Ira Goldenberg describes the views of one sort of detractor:

> ... the T-group is a "game," a "cop-out," however intellectually rationalized and scientifically fortified it might appear. For this group of critics, sensitivity training represents little more than the cultivation of those palaverous skills which allow, indeed enable and reward, people who might otherwise seek to create real social change to live with the status quo and to accept their own impotence and powerlessness with a modicum of dignity. (Goldenberg, 1971, p. 155)

To such critics, who are usually advocates of abrupt social change, the T-group represents an insidious technique that takes the teeth out of social protest by helping people "find themselves," "feel happier," or "be at peace." In this way they envision the potentially militant social change agent metamorphosed through the group process into a latterday Ferdinand the Bull, content to sit in the backyard of social reality and smell the flowers.

In sharp contrast, the intensive group experience has been harshly attacked by right-wing and reactionary groups as "Communist inspired," and a device of "psychological warfare." An article in the November 1967 issue of *Law and Order* magazine warns police chiefs that "sensitivity training" advocated for police department and other public officials represents "ideological war against the entire warp and woof of the American culture." An article in *American Opinion*, the official organ of the John Birch Society (January 1968, p. 73), is descriptively entitled: "'Hate Therapy' Sensitivity Training for Planned Change." In the *Congressional Record-House*, June 10, 1969, a severe diatribe against "Sensitivity Training" spans thirteen pages with analogies to Bolshevistic brainwashing.

An Illustrative Case

In the authors' opinion, the best reply to various critics of groups, and the best means of concretizing the preceding presentations of T-group theory, is through an illustrative case. Our hope is that in the case that follows the reader will see, in the concrete interactions of specific people, an application of the concepts and theories of Rogers, Bennis and Shepard, and others we have already considered in more abstract terms. The particular case selected traces the parallel progress of two members of a self-analytic group for adolescents offered by one of the authors (Stuart Pizer), along with his coleader Dr. Barbara Massar,[2] as a credit course at an elite private preparatory school for boys in New England (which here shall be renamed "The Dickens School"). The T-group course at Dickens, called the Human Relations Seminar, met twice weekly for 1½ hours during each ten-week term of the 1970–71 academic year, and included a list of readings about groups, personality, and psychological issues relevant to adolescents. Students wrote three papers, which the coleaders returned with extensive comments (often an instructor's response would run three or more pages); these papers

---

[2] An earlier version of this case, coauthored by Barbara Massar and Stuart Pizer, appears in Massar (1972) and in Pizer (1972).

were about the student's recollections of what it was like to grow up in his family, who he felt he was now, what he experienced in the group, and what he observed and understood about other group members. The coleaders of the Human Relations Seminar were conducting an extensive research study of group interaction and adolescent growth and learning, which will be described further after the presentation of the case. The research design called for all Human Relations Seminar participants each term to be interviewed and tested before and after their group experience, and for a random sample of Dickens seniors to be identically researched as a control.

Winston Wright and Joshua Rubens both answered the call, in the fall of 1970, for Dickens students to participate in a psychology department study of "The Dickens Student Today." Subsequently, both Winston and Joshua joined the spring term Human Relations Seminar. Neither of them was aware that his participation in the T-group disqualified him as a fall term control group subject in the research study. However, although they were no longer included in the statistical sample, they continued to be interviewed and tested along with the other spring term Human Relations Seminar members. Selections from Winston and Joshua's research interviews, as well as from the papers they wrote for the T-group course, will help augment the segments of group process that illustrate their progress, and growth, through the group experience.

It will soon be clear that Winston and Joshua have been chosen for the case presented here not only because they well represent the kinds of learning and growth possible for participants in intensive group experiences but also because their dramatically contrasting social values and political views, their opposing attitudes toward social change, and the impact of the group experience on their prior social allegiances nicely reply to the criticisms of T-groups as enchanting islands of diversion from social change or subversive schools of revolutionary social change.

Winston Wright dresses in traditional prep school fashion and keeps his hair closely cropped. In his pregroup interview, he expressed his hopes and goals in terms of a career in the "Sciences in general ... biology ... biochemistry ... research...." And also:

> I want to serve some time in the military. I know this is an outmoded feeling, but ... this country has given me quite a bit—and I

feel that I owe something to it. And I don't want to feel like the world owes me a living. It's in the military that you learn to get along with people.

It is important to note here that we do not wish to quarrel with Winston's desire to serve his country. The point we wish to make is that, upon entering the Human Relations Seminar, Winston's hopes and goals are not yet differentiated to the degree that they form *his own* personal ideology. He still maintains his childhood illusion of the infallibility of the family ideology on which he depends. For example, he elaborates, as follows, on why one learns to get along with people in the military:

> I want to go to a college that has ROTC because I want to experience something that my father experienced. I would like to learn something like this. I would like to take ROTC because I know it held my father in good stead.... My father's war experiences have stood him in good stead all the time.

Hence, Winston Wright, at the time of his fall interview, defended his family's system of values against the challenge of his peers in the following way:

> I owe my allegiance to my country. . . . I'm definitely biased against some students by appearance—I feel a definite antagonism. I don't like other people because they disagree with my beliefs. They flaunt . . . they want to tear down everything I believe. They're a dangerous influence. There are some I feel a definite contempt for. . . . I'm concerned to have this country continue as it is. . . . We have a problem with these militants. . . . I don't care if they go ahead and protest all they want, as long as they do this in a fashion . . . in a fashion in which they don't bother me.

Joshua Rubens, who characterized himself as "a Jewish long-haired liberal," whose hopes and goals are expressed in terms of a career in "the social science field," who would soon take his place opposite Winston in the spring Seminar and face him directly with the full force of an alternate ideology, was just such a "dangerous influence." Joshua fancies himself the spokesman for a radical ideology on which he depends with the same ferocity as Winston adheres to the conservative beliefs of his family.

He would most certainly "bother" Winston. Similarly, Winston would most certainly bother him. When Joshua was asked, in the fall interview, "What's it like for you when you feel competent—like when you've done an especially good job?", Joshua replies:

> Satisfied. And kind of . . . you can kind of *sneer* at other people. And kind of a feeling of power. . . . Like last year, my political power at the school, and you know, getting kicked out for quasi-political activities—you know what I mean. And just kind of . . . you've stirred up all these other people's emotions and they come out through you. And like . . . I had 600 people, just dangling at the end of my thumb . . . at my high school last year. It's just a *fantastic* feeling. . . . Or winning that debate trophy. . . . Or when I got accepted at this school as a senior. I was sick that day—when I got that letter, man—I remember, it was 9:02 in the morning when the mail came. And man, I was *better for the rest of the month*!!! . . . when I got accepted. I know it will be that way if I get accepted at the college I want to go to, too. I love challenges . . . like my political activities at my old high school just seemed funny to me. These people are so incompetent . . . you know . . . running around, playing this game. *And I was able to make the rules* . . . and that . . . you know . . . and that . . . you gotta be careful when you're doing that cause you can really mess up a lot of people . . . or yourself.
>
> So . . . when you're running other people. . . . And like . . . my Dad and I would sit down and talk about that for hours on end. I'm sure glad he was there to guide me, cause there were times when I needed it. And, ummm . . . if . . . I don't know . . . "competence" . . . I just feel satisfied. And again, I'll admit it—kind of a sneering feeling at the multitudes . . . the absurd multitudes. . . . But it's a good feeling.

Whereas Winston believes in joining the team, supporting authority, and preserving the traditions of the larger group, Joshua fancies himself the prophet of "the multitudes," bringing the Word to the Land of the Preppies, and personally leading the forces of change. Winston's attitude of unquestioning loyalty and self-sacrifice contrasts dramatically with Joshua's self-seeking and defiant rebelliousness.

Thus, on the surface, and at the manifest level of their thoughts and values, Winston and Joshua appear to come from opposite poles as they enter the spring term Seminar. But, they are essentially alike in their common need for acceptance and approval, and their common fear of rejection or disapproval.

Winston remarks:

Probably the worst thing I can think of, is the fear . . . and it's a very real fear . . . that, uhh, I won't get accepted at the college where I really want to go. And along that line . . . uh . . . at certain times I feel, with some of my classmates, for a certain reason . . . just a little chance thing . . . such as, uhh, how we're walking along at a time like this. And, uh, I say "hello" and he doesn't say "hello" to me—this sort of thing. And I'll begin to wonder why he didn't say hello back. And that sort of thing. But uh, generally . . . *I do not feel that I am any part of a real group.* I can't say that I'm a real part of a group. And this sort of *feeling* I don't like . . . wondering, maybe, how your classmates—what your classmates think about you . . . and, uh, if they like you or not—this sort of thing.

And Joshua says:

I guess most of all . . . I sit there or stand there—or whatever—and wait for acceptance . . . and kind of fear rejection.

And, on the subject of loneliness, Joshua reflects:

Loneliness is a Down. You want so *badly* to be with someone. I guess loneliness abounds for everyone . . . it makes me ask myself, "Why am I me?" It's a good feeling to be accepted by people . . . feeling like people are happy to have you around . . . be accepted by other people. Acceptance and rejection play such a big part in our lives.

In spite of their obvious differences, perhaps it is this basic kinship of needs that will lead Winston and Joshua to discover each other in group interaction.

Fourteen students joined the spring term Seminar. The seeds of counterdependent rebellion were sown in the first meeting by Burbank, who broke the initial silence by asking the coleaders whether they had any objections to his smoking. Even after he had stated—mid-session—

that he happened to be a nonsmoker himself, the group continued to debate the issue of cigarette smoking. Joshua allied himself with the most verbal group members—Burbank, Dan, Alex, and Nick—who interspersed rhetorical arguments for each student's "inalienable right" to smoke, with lengthy diatribes against school rules. More dependent members—Martin, Jay, and Chris—although less forceful in their remarks, addressed the coleaders with veiled requests for them to establish a direction the group could follow. And, Joshua, whose response to conflict is a combination of defiant rebelliousness and open dependency, allied himself with this group also. He said:

> Well, you carry the authority of at least enforcing school rules and handing out grades. So if nothing else, that seems to involve . . . you know . . . answering a question like that [Martin's question about what direction to take] and . . . [you should] *try to pull us out of whatever blindness we're in* . . . in this course, or about you . . . *or about anything*!!

While Stan and Mike pleaded for a more positive attitude in the group, Andrew, Tim, and Henry said nothing at all. Winston participated actively in this meeting, asking constructive questions of others; but, he stood unsupported in his acceptance of school rules and the group's coleaders. At one point, Winston softly inquired:

> What would happen if, instead of worrying about the school rules, a member in the group . . . or the group turned around and said: "Please don't smoke." Would you follow that directive?

With an audible sigh of disdain, Joshua turned his head heavenward. Winston's inquiry was dropped. As the first meeting came to a close, Burbank and his coalition established what they believed to be a general consensus: that high hopes for the success of this group had been dashed. Members were all deeply disappointed. It was, after all, abundantly clear that interpersonal relationships could not possibly be established in a setting under the jurisdiction of the school and its rules.

Winston, whose characteristic response to conflict has been withdrawal, absents himself from session II.

Session III, joined by Bob (a new member), concerned itself with caring in the group. To begin with, dependent members asked the coleaders if they thought people cared in the group, and counterdependent members said that they did not care:

MARTIN: Do you think the silence means that we don't care?
NICK: I don't care about this group. I feel indifferent. If certain members left, it wouldn't make any difference to me. If I left, it wouldn't make any difference to me.

Jay's attempt to engage Dan in conversation is met with rebuff. Group members begin to voice their opinions of various types of people—northerners, southerners, jocks, freaks. Then, the group effects a resolution of differences by joining together in scapegoating the school. Winston is silent.

BOB: Dickens is a hostile community. It's not like home.
CHRIS: Home is a special place.
BARBARA: I think that the place that's familiar . . . the place where you're accustomed to customs, the place where you know how you'll be reacted to—is a place where you may feel like one of the home folks.
JAY: Yeah. There's an Academy accent around here. And . . . so many different people from so many different parts. How can anyone feel comfortable?

At this juncture, Stuart attempts to relate the feelings of discomfort back into the group. He observes that Winston, who has not yet spoken in the meeting, seemed to nod in assent to Jay's last statement. But Stuart is ignored and the scapegoating of the school turns to an attack on Jay for objecting to different kinds of people. Once more, opinions of "good" and "bad" and "right" and "wrong" begin to fly across the room. Then Stuart interjects:

STUART: I think we need to distinguish between opinions and feelings. And the thing is, if an opinion is attacked, a person assumes his feelings have been attacked. And the irony of that is—opinions are often expressed to protect one's feelings. That is, a person comes to present his feelings in the form of an opinion. And so, then he gets attacked. And therefore he expects his

BURBANK: feelings to be attacked. And it goes on and on like that.
But opinions are, relatively speaking, easy to voice. But it's very hard to explain an emotion. Opinions ... umm ... their very nature is that they're definable in words. But emotion, you cannot define. So it's kind of hard to say, "here's my feeling," and *explain* it. Explain it so that anyone can understand what the hell you're talking about. But you can express a feeling through ... I don't know.

[Silence]

BARBARA: Perhaps there is feeling expressed in the silence now.
BURBANK: The best feelings I feel are umm ... the most important feelings to me are the ones that cannot be put into words. Maybe that's why I find the silence so interesting.

Once more, Joshua straddles the fence between the dependent and the counterdependent groups. After a prolonged silence, he says:

I could be a lot freer if we could do what we wanted. I'd like to have a cigarette right now.

And Winston remains *entirely* silent throughout the meeting. At the close of session III, Barbara says:

The thing that's important for us to recognize, and to realize is that feeling, and the expression of feeling, may draw us together. And there may be two things going on today in the group: the desire to draw together, and the desire to pull apart. Two feelings at the same time. I have a feeling that that's what we are struggling with in here.

In session IV, the group continues its preoccupation with issues of authority, control, and dependency. Joshua actively asserts his ideals and his individualism. Winston struggles to preserve his own individuality by silent withdrawal from confrontation with a threatening viewpoint.

The following is an excerpt from session IV.

JOSHUA: How come when you're eighteen years old, you're old enough to kill? Can anybody explain that?
CHRIS: Why?
JOSHUA: Well the fact that on one day . . . one day we're old enough to vote for Mr. Nixon . . . and kill some people cause their skins are a different color than ours . . . *just like that*!

[Silence]

JOSHUA: It's hard for me to figure out what all that means, cause I don't have any concept of really killing, I guess.
MARTIN: Do you expect an answer, or are you speaking rhetorically?
STAN: Probably young people make better soldiers.
STUART: [reflectively] Joshua, you said two things today. You didn't read further in Carl Rogers cause you didn't want to know what was going to happen in here. Then you talked about growing up . . . about being told to kill.

[Silence]

For much of this session, the interaction centers on forms of attack, killing, and dying. Confrontations between group members are verbalized in terms of political arguments and geographical differences. When Jay asserts that he could die for his country, Dan—offended by Jay's remark in session III about southerners—condemns the "my country right or wrong attitude," as well as the notion of dying for freedom, as "just a lot of shit." Joshua leads a subgroup of students who propose the necessity for revolution.

During the last half hour of the meeting, Winston has put his head down on the table. His gesture is overtly ignored by the group, until Barbara draws attention to him. When the group perceives Barbara's comment to Winston as a teacher's reprimand, Joshua, who still considers himself the antithesis of everything that Winston stands for, leaps to his defense. Joshua's first gesture toward Winston is an indirect one, based on his assumption that Winston has become an oppressed minority in the group. And, Joshua sees himself as the leader of all who are oppressed. As the discussion develops, Winston begins to verbalize his feelings of apartness, insularity, and vulnerability to rejection by the group. Joshua, despite his differences of *opinion*, begins to identify with Winston's *feelings* of isolation, and also admires his courage to express his feelings to the group.

Joshua's feeling of admiration may be seen as the first glimmerings, for him, of respect for one of "the multitudes." Perhaps it was Winston's courage, as well as his vulnerability, that inspired Joshua, at the end of the meeting, to make a statement advocating recognition across differences. Although Joshua's professed belief may not reflect an understanding that he has actually internalized and integrated in his relationship with others, his statement in session IV constitutes his public commitment to that aspiration.

We continue the excerpt from session IV at the point of Barbara's comment to Winston:

BARBARA: Winston, I wonder whether it's possible for you to express what you're expressing.

WINSTON: I'm expressing? Uh. I just had a headache—that's why I put my head down. That's the only reason. I haven't been feeling too well. So that's why I haven't said much in here.

BARBARA: I didn't ask you not to feel it.

WINSTON: Yeah. Right.

ALEX: It's incredible the fear Dickens students have. . . . Incredible. Really terror. And they get used to it. . . . And they think it's common courtesy.

DAN: [to Barbara] Maybe that's your way of asking him not to do it.

BARBARA: Is that a way you've become accustomed to around here—for people to make requests?

ALEX: Well they do it in very odd ways.

[Group Laughter]

DAN: Well . . . [group laughter] I know, but every time you make a comment about something it . . . it's immediately reacted to. . . . So whether you *intend* it that way or not . . . it . . . it becomes a request in effect.

JOSHUA: I'm curious why you asked Winston that—cause—cause I was asleep for awhile too—probably for completely different reasons, but I . . . I was curious why you asked Winston. And I'm *directing that right to you*!!!

BARBARA: I think that other people as well as myself were concerned in some way . . . and did not want Winston *not* to put his head down . . . but it seemed like a message that I found difficult to understand . . . to respond to . . . and it expressed something. It expressed the headache, but I didn't know. I wanted to know whether he would share what it expressed . . . which was interpreted by some as a "correction" in a round about way. Like asking him not to do it. . . . That's true, there are familiar ways of responding—like at Dickens as Alex said. So if another figure in your lives—like in early childhood—or when you're older—or wherever—doesn't talk to you directly and give you a direct message—then we may tend to feel we are suspected and accused.

STUART: The meaning for each person who receives a message always has partly to do with the message—and partly to do with what it means in your own personal universe.

WINSTON: Alex, I'm curious about your interpretation of my reaction. Do you think that the reason I rose my head was because of terror?

[Silence]

MIKE: No . . . I really would say the look in your face . . . was one in a . . . a look of being startled.

WINSTON: Well, I'll confess I was falling asleep also. The reason I arose my head was to stay awake. So, I mean, it was not a matter of terror.

BARBARA: Is that a requirement? Do you sense or feel a requirement in here to stay awake?

WINSTON: Well . . . it's not just a matter of staying awake or falling asleep . . . it's a feeling that you're now . . . when you're weak, or something like this, in a class . . . it's a feeling that you could be called upon at any time . . . it's just a feeling that you're not prepared. It's a feeling like . . . I have to keep up my defenses or something . . . kind of . . . uh . . . if I get caught unawares . . . and I've got my defenses down low. . . .

STUART: Even though this isn't a class where there are daily recitations and assignments . . . perhaps there are feelings in here of not being prepared for what's going on.

As Bob said before—ummm—in fact what I believe you're in a sense elaborating on is the feeling of . . . the difficulty sometimes of coping with what is going on—perhaps understanding it—of connecting it . . . of knowing where you fit in . . . and uh . . . there are a lot of ways of dealing with that. One is to struggle with that—sometimes painful experience—that feeling. Or *it may be* to withdraw . . . to get bored . . . or to, uh . . . in a sense, to become silent.

[Silence]

WINSTON: I'll start off and say why I've been silent. And uh . . . well, I feel like I can say now. It's because some of these issues we were discussing—are very controversial . . . and uh . . . important to me. And some of my beliefs are definitely contrary to what the majority of the group thinks as . . . and I frankly do not want to uh . . . I guess . . . take that chance that my beliefs will be refuted and cause doubt in my own mind . . . because I have been under a serious . . . uh . . . doubt for quite some time. And I really just didn't want to take the chance that anybody was going to add fuel to the fire, so to speak. So that's why I have been listening—but I have not been saying anything, cause I imagine some of my views could be rebutted fairly easily—and I would be even more insecure than I feel right now.

STUART: I think sometimes in saying something very personal— a person can speak for a lot of others as well. And I guess in a more general sense I heard you say that there are risks in here; that it *is* risky business to offer something of yourself to other people in a way in which . . . uhh . . . you could get disagreement . . . uhh . . . you could get ignored.

WINSTON: [agreeing] Uh-huh.

STUART: Or you could see alternatives that are so striking that —uhh—it makes you question yourself.

WINSTON: Yeah. That's the thing that bothers me most, I think. . . . Well, to give you an idea—I particularly noticed

> hostility toward Jay, and uh, Jay and I share more ... very similar beliefs—and I noticed that he was being ... that there was more hostility towards him and that people were attacking what he saw and believed in. And so the arguments began to make me think. And uh ... well I guess I wanted to think more. ... If something is contrary to what I believe in—I've got to shut up completely ... but uh ... I was sympathizing with Jay and what he said and uh ... well to say ... to attack someone—I didn't want to open myself up to the same position—because I felt I was just a minority.

Toward the end of the meeting, Winston elaborates further:

> WINSTON: I didn't consider myself as part of the group and I'll say right now—I think subconsciously—maybe even consciously—I've been fighting this thing all along the whole way because ... you know, like how are we going to open you up—yourself up in a certain case. And there are certain things that I just don't want anybody to know. So maybe that's why I've been fighting it all along. And—putting my head down. Well I did have a headache and that sort of thing too—but it was also a way of just sort of being a little more insular and staying what I am. And not contributing to the group.
>
> [Silence]
>
> BOB: I bet you—everyone feels that way somehow.
> ANDREW: Yeah. Me too.
> BOB: Cause it just opens you up, I think. Stuart mentioned that earlier—opening yourself up for the goods—you're making yourself more vulnerable ... it's kind of. ...
>
> [Silence]
>
> STUART: It's risky. And I think there's some fear in here of ... uh ... perhaps each person fears his destructive power. His power to hurt someone else by reacting in a sense —by ... starting out communication. And the beginning of communication is to recognize where you are —and where someone else is ... and communicate

across those differences. And there are a lot of differences in here: differences of South and North ... differences of race ... differences of values ... differences of sex ... just differences in style.

[Silence]

JOSHUA: Is communication a way of understanding those differences? Or resolving them? Because to me it's like —uh—the most that I usually—personally will remember—and that I view—you know—in terms of relationship with people ... when I come to ... *not to resolve* their differences and reconcile theirs with mine—and try to make them think the way *I* do or anything, but I guess rather, those are—you know—are the people that *I really understand*. I mean that what's always been more meaningful to me ... and ... if I look back over the people whom I called friends, or girls that I liked or were in love with or whatever ... and the very few who really stand out as being close to me—it seems like ... you know ... I just *knew* that ... and *understood* them ... and was able to *comprehend* what they believed in and how they saw me or whatever. I don't know, it just seems an indication of....

BARBARA: Are you talking to Stuart or are you talking to Winston?

JOSHUA: Anybody that wants to listen. It's just that—Stuart motivated the thought ... like him saying that ... you know ... a communication is to recognize—and then to build from there. And it's just ... you know ... the way I guess I felt. But the *recognition* I think is really important. And it always has been for me.

BARBARA: If through some kind of openness we can understand our differences, I think that's important. But also, I just want to stress again what was in the Gendlin article we read. Each of us do have—also—our desire for some kind of privacy ... and that your communication and your sharing with us your feelings, will help us to help you to keep the things inside that you want to keep inside—as well.

[Silence ... birds chirping ...]

STUART: I think we'll stop for today.

In Joshua's second paper, which he chose to write about Winston, he reflects:

> Winston and I had the same English course Winter term and he never said anything like that. I think what also binds me to Winston is his honesty and openness in the group. Perhaps he feels open to attack when he is open like that, and I, too, often feel open to attack for opening up too much. Or it could be that he feels much of the loneliness that runs through my body and head, especially after having opened myself up for expressing a view; or when I was on trial for _____ with Dean _____ and _____.

Although, by session VI, Joshua is able to recognize the meaning of openness as far as others are concerned, his own openness is still apprehended in terms of expressing views and taking an activist stance at the school. And, by session VI, his flamboyant speeches in assembly (Joshua had been elected president of the Co-op, the student government at Dickens) had indeed gotten him into serious trouble with the faculty and administration. In session VI, acceptance and rejection is once more the major focus in the group—on this day particularly, since the letters of acceptance or rejection from colleges have just arrived that morning. But Joshua's acceptance in the college of his choice is diminished for him in the light of his current trial with Dickens. And now it is Winston who identifies with the feelings Joshua haltingly unfolds. For, as observed earlier, although Winston and Joshua differ at the manifest level of their thoughts and values, they are essentially alike in their common vulnerability to rejection or disapproval. Whereas Joshua was in jeopardy for opposing school rules in blatant rebellion, Winston had been threatened by faculty members in an earlier year for his overzealous adherence to the traditional role of a Dickens man. As Winston described that time in his pregroup interview:

> Mr. _____ told me I'd made a very good try here, but that the administration didn't expect me to make it. They didn't expect me to succeed ... I was stunned by this ... I thought that I had been betrayed by everybody. And I guess it was right after I had just finished having mononucleosis at that point so I was in a particularly dejected period. I didn't go home and slash my wrists or anything, but ... uh ... I just felt *terrible*. It was ... because of

this one little incident . . . and everybody was convinced that I was
a failure . . . and I went home, and I wrote a long letter to my
father . . . and I never sent it. [Laugh] I decided I wouldn't send
it . . . I'd wait on it . . . and think things over because I knew if I
sent it, he'd probably take me out of school, for one thing. Well,
I decided that's not what I wanted. My father came up a couple of
times that year . . . and kept asking me whether they [family] could
have possibly made a mistake . . . whether Dickens was the right
place for me or not . . . and I was so *mad* at this point, that I
decided I was going to stick it out anyhow. And I went through that
year. And then . . . they hit me with that wonderful letter which I
wasn't supposed to open. It was addressed to my father . . . in which
Mr. _____ and Mr. _____ recommended that
they look for another school for me . . . *because they considered
that I was striving too high,* and that I was *not* happy, and uh . . . I
was just . . . you know . . . *who can be a judge of my happiness.*
Now that is something that infuriated me also. Just because Mr.
_____ thought I was *working* too hard, grinding all the
time, or studying—he was convinced I wasn't happy. Now maybe
. . . if I was getting '5's' and '6's' in my courses—which I was at the
time—*that made me happy.* That was *my* happiness. But he was
convinced I wasn't. And that was another point in which I was
lonely.

As session VI begins, group members communicate alternate expressions of anger and disdain for the "college game." Some of the silent members seem visibly upset. Stories of friends receiving rejection letters are related. More anger is released. Then:

BARBARA: I feel like we're having some difficulty acknowledging some feelings of sadness in here. Maybe . . . in ye olde prep school it's even more difficult, you know, when somebody feels bad. What is the right thing to say?
MIKE: What you're talking about, Barbara, is one of the most real feelings that I've encountered in my years here . . . just the lack of feeling for anybody else.
BARBARA: Is it really a lack of *feeling*? Or does it have to do with some unspoken rules . . . about Dickens Men? Is it a fear, or inability to express? I don't know.
STAN: Inability. Not knowing a means. It would be unheard of to embrace somebody here. Or say you cared.

STUART: Then you do know a means.
STAN: Unheard of . . . that's strange.
STUART: The way you could express; would that be strange?
WINSTON: Especially if you don't know how the person's going to react either.
MIKE: It's awkward to be misunderstood.
JAY: The last thing somebody wants is pity.
BARBARA: For me there is a difference between caring and pity. I mean, feeling bad *for* somebody . . . and feeling bad *with* somebody.

[Silence]

BOB: There's a heavy weight in here. Feels morbid. I know it's going to pass.
STUART: I think this is a shared day of emotional importance. Today is one of those shared days in which people seem to be becoming more isolated from each other. It . . . it's a very lonely thing.
JOSHUA: Well . . . it took the drive out of me. I found out from all the schools I applied to last week. Early. But . . . it's just like somebody had kinda . . . turned down the steam or something . . . because I really don't give a shit about this place now. I thought, I mean really seriously, about just . . . you know . . . fucking it and going home . . . going back to _____ and going to school there for the rest of the year. Instead of worrying here about getting kicked out. And knowing that Mr. _____ is watching over his boys nightly and everything . . . you know . . . and just . . . and then . . . well . . . I really had an unpleasant experience in terms of competence with a teacher. I guess that didn't help. But . . . uh . . . you know . . . I'm in there and I really don't give a damn—about being here at Dickens now.

[Silence]

JOSHUA: [continues] And it was really . . . I guess it was really several things coupled together . . . but . . . it's hard for me to accept that because . . . this is so great a school in terms of education that I just never have been able to get before . . . and I *wanted* it. It was a challenge and I really liked it. But . . . maybe the challenge has ended . . . or . . . there's something, I don't know, but I'm just ready to, you know, say to hell with it and go home.

In this case, Joshua communicated feelings in the group: feelings that Winston had saved up for a long, long time, feelings Winston had experienced in the privacy of his dormitory room and had communicated in a letter to his father that he never sent.

In Joshua's second paper, he writes:

And then after the meeting where I expressed my anger and rage at what Dean _____ and _____ did to me, Winston came up afterwards and put his arm on my shoulder and said something to the effect of "Take care of yourself, Joshua." What a human, simple, beautiful thing to do. But outside of brief, yet strongly emotional moments such as this we never really get together or talk or anything.

By the following week, political unrest at the school has mounted, and five of the group's participants are absent from session VIII. Members are uncertain as to the whereabouts of Alex, Dan, Burbank, and Joshua; and Stuart announces that Barbara is in bed with the flu.

In the space left by the absent members, Winston assumes a new role for himself, one of outspoken leadership. He becomes a spokesman for diversity and caring in the group. Thus, Winston now takes up the banner raised by Joshua in session IV when he had advocated recognition and friendship across differences. Indeed, Winston accepts the banner like a true activist, a social gadfly, as he admonishes the group:

BOB: Everything . . . happens *after* the meeting.
WINSTON: How come you can't bring it out in here!? Why isn't this atmosphere conducive to what we're trying to do?
BOB: What are we trying to do?
WINSTON: *Care about the group!!* That's a goal!

Other group members resist openness and caring in the group. Bob suggests that some people may talk too much, and cites Joshua as his example, which arouses criticism of Joshua from several of the more silent group members.

> WINSTON: I don't think we're necessarily . . . you *have to* care for . . . uhh . . . if Joshua comes up with a point of view that you don't agree with, there's nothing wrong in that. I mean, you can have your own point of view also . . . but, there's no reason to reject it entirely—or to reject him.

And, later:

> WINSTON: Of course, we don't want to lose our individuality entirely . . . but that doesn't mean we have to set ourselves apart—outside the group. . . . The group can encourage the individual . . . just not an individual set apart from the group.

Joshua returns in session IX. Now, his progress in the group beyond a state of dependent-counterdependent fluctuation—between reliance upon authority and revolt—and his approach toward awareness of the meaning of interdependent relationships, is reflected in his statement:

> It's different in here. Here . . . unless each person *gives* something . . . *there won't be anything!* As when. . . . That's not the way it usually is . . . uh. . . . We're not usually asked to give anything. We're just asked to take and to accept. And I think it's so much better when people can give something that they have within them . . . and build something out of that. . . . Build trust or build a group or build a discussion or whatever. I mean, I would really feel bad if this was in a regular classroom because I would . . . I would feel . . . *Underneath.* And I really don't here. I don't feel Underneath at all. I feel . . . equal. And that's about the best feeling I like to have.

Joshua's statement suggests that, no longer needing to rely upon defiant rebelliousness, he is able to articulate to the group his appreciation of mutual cooperation in an interdependent relationship with equals. However, this progress of Joshua's does not yet transfer beyond the group. On the Dickens campus, with the inexorable snowballing of student protests in which Joshua had been a pivotal leader, he was being carried along by the momentum of events that threatened him with serious trouble.

By session XI, Joshua and Winston are communicating with each other quite *directly in the group*—with warmth, good humor, and genuine support. Now, in this meeting, which marks the breakthrough of mutuality in Winston's and Joshua's relationship, it becomes impossible to distinguish which aspects of their rapport are an outcome of the dissolution of stereotypes and the creation of empathy through group interaction, and which aspects reflect a recognition of the basic *similarity* of their egocentric origins at a moment of new growth. For as Piaget has also made clear:

> The phenomenon [adolescent egocentricity] is the same whether it has to do with the misunderstood and anxious youngster convinced of failure [Winston] or with the active youngster convinced of his own genius [Joshua]. (Piaget, 1968, p. 66)

It seems crucial to add that, within a day of session XI, Winston arrived at the office of the school psychologist for his second voluntary interview. His responses to questions concerning his present feelings about his classmates, and the ways in which he now perceives himself as different from them, are as follows:

> I have mixed feelings about some of the issues they are very, very concerned about. Uhh . . . since my last interview with you, I have definitely changed, I think. I would not consider I have gotten . . . radical, or anything like this but . . . I find now that I'm willing to listen . . . but *now* these thoughts don't just pass through my mind for me to say, "Well, they're wrong, but that's their thing if they want to do it that way." Uhh . . . things which I hold very close to me, which are very important to me . . . this year has caused me to doubt some of these things—such as some of my moral values . . . uh . . . the way I feel about certain things . . . uh . . . my whole attitude toward . . . uh . . . oh, the *country* and this sort of thing. And, as I say, I have been *listening* to these people and I *think* sometimes —which I don't think I really considered that much before—but I think sometimes they have a legitimate grievance. . . .

And Winston continues:

> . . . a very legitimate grievance. I have mixed feelings of my own . . . and I really don't know which . . . which are correct anymore . . .

you know . . . I can't put them down. It's . . . uh . . . a *transition* for me. . . .

Winston concludes:

> . . . a transition . . . in which I have thoughts which are very, very important to me, which have been almost innate . . . ingrained thoughts . . . responses that I've grown up with all my life. . . . And finally to be *confronted* with these other thoughts which—after some consideration—do seem reasonable . . . well it makes things difficult.

In session XI, Winston and Joshua's clear communication—not only to each other, but to the whole group—of their transition from confrontation to mutual support, allows other group members as well to participate in a process of illuminating and comprehending the various restrictive family ideologies, or alternative systems of belief from which they, too, need to emerge for the sake of greater individual freedom.

In this meeting, Joshua begins to talk about the fears he has ("I feel there are definitely some people on campus who would like to see my presence eliminated"), about the loneliness that he experiences at school, and about his need to be able to trust somebody. Other group members share these feelings. The talk shifts to home and close family ties. Some students compare their mistrust of Dickens faculty members with their implicit trust in their parents at home. At this point, Winston, moved by Joshua's pain, relates to the group how he had confided in his parents at a time of his own severe stress. He had disclosed to them feelings of deep depression, isolation, and hopelessness (which will not be detailed here). Indeed, it was this very incident, cited by Winston in session IV, that he never wanted anybody else to know. For Winston to share with a group of his peers deeply personal and confidential matters which, until then, he had entrusted only to his parents, is an important step for him. And, when Winston completes his soft-spoken and ungarnished account, the group is moved to silence. Joshua rubs his eyes.

BARBARA: I think, Winston, you have been the spokesman for trust today. We've been talking about trust all term, and we talked about it again today, and you trusted us.

Outside the group, rumors of possible violence still persist on campus, and threats escalate.

Joshua is absent from session XII. He has sequestered himself in the infirmary with a case of mononucleosis. It is tempting to speculate that, outside the group, Joshua was becoming more ambivalent, more conflicted, about his part in the powder keg of "revolutionary" melodrama. Perhaps he had already crossed the Rubicon among the campus zealots, and felt that he could no longer extricate himself. In any event, he seems to have entered at that time a transitional phase in which he was too aware of a fuller reality to act impulsively, and too overextended or committed to abjure his radical position. What was he to do? It is perhaps understandable that what Joshua now did was to contract mononucleosis, as Winston had done two years earlier. So, Joshua was out of commission, and out of trouble.

In his infirmary room, Joshua continued to listen to the tapes of group sessions. When he returned to the group, he wrote a final paper only one page in length, in which he said, "I can't explain how close I felt to Winston." Barbara and Stuart returned the paper and asked him to try again. At the next group meeting, Joshua submitted a half-sheet of paper, on which he indicated his ordeal in summoning the effort to explicate what he felt he had to say. Barbara sent him a note:

> Won't you please try to fulfill the written requirement of the course that we agreed on? We believe it is important for *you* to carry through work that (you say) is meaningful to you.
>
> If we can be of additional help—don't hesitate to call us.

In the paper Joshua then sent to Barbara and Stuart (titled "And We Try Again . . .") he wrote:

> The underlying tie [between Winston and me] is probably a mixture of all these common traits or feelings. They can be totalled up to some kind of alienation, or it is that Winston and I have and share many of the same goals, wishes, prayers and desires in life. But each of us has chosen a different course to attain those goals, or ideals, or it could be that both Winston and myself feel a strong need to interact with people that isn't always fulfilled. I am not sure that I have exactly put my finger on it but I believe at the core of each of us there's something very similar and nearly alike. . . .

> I hope that in some way my expressing feelings that were (and are) very close to me helped Winston in some way bring himself to terms with opening up and breaking down walls.

Significantly, for Joshua, "breaking down the walls" now has come to mean, not the destruction of institutions, but the relief of isolation by removing internal barriers to intimacy. Later in his paper, Joshua concludes:

> Winston was a major factor in my becoming conscious of what the idea of the encounter group was about. His lead was translated in my head to start looking for significance in what people say and do. Since only last week this has come to be a conscious factor in the way I try to understand people.
> I have changed. I feel I have grown. I feel I have learned.
> I believe a large part of this can be attributed to an accidental yet crucial fact, that being Winston's participation in the group.

Applications and Implications of Groups

Psychological Education The Human Relations Seminar at Dickens School, from which the case of Winston and Joshua was drawn, is a self-analytic group course designed specifically to be conducive to adolescent growth and learning. Several beliefs about high school education, about adolescence, and about T-groups provided the basis for this academic undertaking at Dickens.

1 Teaching need not be in rote form, with students required to accept fact or theory on the basis of the teacher's authority. A T-group setting can provide firsthand experience that makes theoretical ideas meaningful and exciting to the student because they are directly relevant to what is happening in the group. Hence, ideas come alive in the group process. Such an academic format is most obviously applicable for the learning of psychological theory; but also is adaptable to other subject areas, such as literature, history, philosophy, etc.

2 Thinking and feeling are not separated in nature. Ideas arouse strong feelings, and emotions are virtually never devoid of content. Hence, the school curriculum need not be dichotomized as *either* academic/cognitive *or* social/affective (as reflected in old-fashioned report cards). The current movement toward deliberate psychological education (see Alschuler, 1969 and Mosher & Sprinthall, 1971) reflects this growing awareness on the part of educators.

3 In a T-group, the student can learn from his peers under the guidance of a teacher, without the rigid authority of the traditional teacher-student relationship. Such considerations will be relevant in Chapter 5 in the discussion of socialization in the schools.

4 Finally, adolescence is a critical time of important processes of personality integration. Piaget (1968) observes adolescence to be the developmental period in which the individual acquires a new capacity for high-level reflective, or "propositional," thought. The intellectual task of adolescence is to integrate this new power of thought so that it may be used, and not abused. Harry Stack Sullivan (1953) has described the adolescent's need to integrate his separate lust, intimacy, and security needs. Further, adolescence is a time of acute conflict over dependence upon the family, and the family's dogma about life versus independence and a personal identity. Hence, adolescence is a time particularly ripe for a T-group experience. The individual student's active engagement in the group process, as the group progressively integrates the complexity of its novel experience, contributes to the internal personality integration of the adolescent student. The T-group, or self-analytic group, experience provides for two essential needs of the developing adolescent: supportive recognition and personal confrontation.

The findings of the research project at Dickens (see Massar, 1972, and Pizer, 1972), referred to earlier, are germane to our discussion here, because they indicate the impact of a self-analytic group experience upon growth and learning in adolescence.

1 During their term in the Seminar, Human Relations group members increased significantly on an interview measure of *experiencing* (see Gendlin, 1967). That is, the individual group member gained access to his own inner feelings and increased his capacity to use his feelings to ask questions about himself and thereby generate continuing self-awareness. Control group members in the research study remained unchanged on these measures during the same period of time.

2 Through their group experience, participants in the Human Relations Seminar increased significantly in an interview measure of *ego relatedness*—that is, awareness of oneself from an internal perspective; recognition and appreciation of a relationship with other people, and awareness of their own separate inner-feeling life; recognition of one's own inner processes of thinking and learning, and a capacity for complex, relativistic and unstereotyped thinking; as well as a capacity for spontaneous new insights about oneself and others.

3 A comparative study of the three papers written by each seminar member over the term revealed an increasing frequency of abstract thinking, inference making beyond the givens of experience, recognition of parts-to-whole relationships, and use of creative symbols and imagery.

Once again, these research findings are relevant to the discussion, in Chapter 5, of socialization in the schools, and the whole question of what kind of adults we seek to develop through our educational practices.

Community Development T-group techniques have been employed to develop manpower resources in underdeveloped communities, or nations. David C. McClelland (see McClelland & Winter, 1969) has combined a theory of motivation with the social engineering techniques of groups, to help activate the economies of rural Indian villages, blacks, communities in Washington, D.C., and impoverished counties in Kentucky. McClelland based his motivation-training programs on the assumption that economies with insufficient financial resources for investment can capitalize on the motivation of people to achieve realistically elevated goals. McClelland and his associates have used small groups, applying specialized games, didactic instruction, and self-analysis, to successfully activate the entrepreneurship of small businessmen, and to train community leaders to be more potent change agents. Similar training programs have operated in such disparate locales as Boston, Curacao, and Mexico.

Intergroup Relations The T-group has been shown to originate from an effort to enhance intergroup relations. Erving Polster (1970) has described a fascinating recent application of group encounter in a Cleveland, Ohio community. He and other staff members from the Cleveland Gestalt Institute visited a coffee gallery at a borderland locale at the nexus of black, working-class, and student communities. Polster ran encounter group sessions at the coffee gallery, employing some techniques of psychodrama, to help members of the various social groups understand more about one another's views of the strains among different communities.

Conflict Resolution One very needed application of small group technique is in the aid of establishing understanding, and perhaps even peace, between openly hostile communities or nations. The case of Winston and Joshua has already demonstrated how an arch-radical and an arch-conservative can mutually recognize their common humanity, and their own wider potentials, through a group encounter. T-groups have been used in the Middle East, with a membership of equal numbers of Israelis and Palestinian Arab refugees, in the interest of creating some new understanding, and the possibility for a collaborative solution to brutal social divisions.

At the time of this writing, a project is under way to conduct an encounter group consisting of Northern Irish Protestants and Catholics, including members of the Irish Republican Army and the British Army. These group sessions are to be filmed, and the final film version of the group distributed for screening in public places in Northern Ireland in the interest of resolving the mistrusts and misunderstandings that have recently lacerated that country. A similar venture of filming an encounter group for wider public observation was highly successful a few years ago. At that time, Carl Rogers ran a group for people concerned about drugs, including drug users, former addicts, and parents of users. The resulting film, distributed as "Journey into Self," is a very moving documentary which won an Academy Award.

Humanization Admittedly a very general term, "humanization" does seem to describe the process of change in organizations that have turned to the use of face-to-face group encounters. For example, in industry, where psychological technology has been exploited for the express purpose of raising production, the group movement has accompanied a growing recognition by many large corporations that the office or factory is a place where employees spend much of their waking day, that labor need not be thoroughly alienated, that workers are more effective if they feel personally attended to, and that the work group is a community (McGregor, 1961). Hence, industry has invested money (the acid test) in programs designed, not to accelerate output, but to make the conditions of work more pleasant and humane.

Many Catholic seminaries and monastic orders in the United States have adopted T-group procedures in their training structure as part of a shifting emphasis away from authority, dogma, and conformity and toward democracy, interaction, and growth. This use of group techniques is producing a quiet revolution in social relations and personal development in formerly rigid social orders that offers hope for change in the kinds of total institutions described in the following chapter.

Chapter 4

Psychology and Change in Institutions

On the morning of September 9, 1971, inmates of the maximum security prison at Attica, New York, seized hostages and barricaded themselves into a cell block, beginning a dramatic five-day protest against prison conditions. The inmates presented a long and varied list of complaints. Among other items, they demanded an end to alleged physical and psychological mistreatment, removal of restrictions on certain forms of political and religious activity, an end to censorship of reading material, payment for labor in prison at the rates specified by the state's minimum wage laws, the right to free communication with people outside the walls, the establishment of grievance procedures through an ombudsman program, and improved food, medical care, and rehabilitative services. The protest came to a bloody end on Monday, September 13, when 1,000 guards, state troopers, and sheriff's deputies from the surrounding counties assaulted and recaptured the prisoners' stronghold. When the assault was over, forty-three men were dead, most of them, prisoners and hostages alike, victims of police bullets.

A different kind of state institution came under a different kind of attack in 1967, when a lawyer and film maker named Frederick Wiseman shocked the state of Massachusetts and the nation with a film called *Titicut Follies,* an unstaged documentary on life at the Bridgewater (Massachusetts) state hospital for the criminally insane. Some of the film's shock effect came from grim scenes of old men herded naked through corridors and locked in barren cells. Ultimately, however, subtler features of human interaction were responsible for the film's impact —extraordinarily callous treatment of inmates by staff and dismal failures of communication between medical personnel and the people they were supposed to help.

It would be comforting to believe that the prison at Attica and the mental hospital at Bridgewater are not typical institutions of their kind and that most of our prisons and mental hospitals are relatively benign. However, there is little evidence to support such a belief. Protests of the kind that occurred at Attica have been frequent in the history of the penal system; muckraking journalists and ex-patients have repeatedly exposed atrocious conditions in the mental hospitals. Perhaps more fundamentally, prisons and mental hospitals are vulnerable to criticism quite aside from these all-too-frequent disclosures of intolerable conditions: the persistence of criminal behavior among many ex-inmates and the wasted lives of mental patients confined in hospitals without effective treatment reflect serious failures of these institutions to achieve their stated goals of beneficial change.

This chapter pursues our theme of psychology and social change in two senses. First, it deals with institutions that are part of society's effort to improve itself by transforming deviant individuals—"rehabilitating" offenders and "curing" the mentally ill. Second, the chapter describes changes now occurring in the institutions themselves, as society alters its beliefs about criminality and mental illness and reevaluates the role of existing institutions in changing people to conform with societal norms.

We can gain some insight into the connections between these institutions and the theme of social change, as well as the psychological assumptions underlying the organization of contemporary prisons and mental hospitals, by a brief look at the history of these institutions. Prisons and mental hospitals, as we now know them, have not always existed. Criminals and "madmen" have been handled very differently in other cultures and other times. In the Middle Ages they were commonly tortured and murdered, although in isolated instances the mentally disturbed were treated more humanely than we generally treat them today. Prisons have of course existed throughout history, and asylums go back at least as far as 1547, when Henry VIII established the institution that came to be known as "Bedlam." But the institutions bearing those names were commonly nothing but cages in which people were chained to walls like animals.

The modern concept of prisons and asylums as settings for reform and cure arose after the French Revolution, with the mental hospital reforms of Philippe Pinel in France and William Tuke in England. In the United States reforms gained momentum with the establishment of new prisons and mental hospitals during the 1830s and 1840s. Criminals and the mentally disturbed had generally been treated in unenlightened fashion in the American colonies, as David Rothman shows in his fascinating history, *The Discovery of the Asylum* (1971). Those of the mentally ill who were without family or friends to care for them were either left to fend for themselves or put in small, local almshouses with other impoverished people. Petty criminals were publicly humiliated through devices such as the stocks; more serious or persistent offenders were whipped, hanged, or often simply exiled. Mental illness was thought to be an affliction of divine or demonic origin, not susceptible to human intervention; crime was the work of the Devil, and a personal moral failing of the individual involved; the criminal might be punished, but if punishment failed, nothing could be done to reform him—hence execution or exile seemed the only courses of action.

With the coming of the new American republic, attitudes changed, and a new optimism prevailed. Crime and mental illness began to be seen as consequences of decadent European society and the evil influence of city life. The new world of freedom and opportunity would surely make such social ills obsolete. Thus, from their very beginnings, prisons and mental hospitals in the United States were linked to social change. They were seen as an integral part of the new and better society.

This Enlightenment belief in the perfectibility of man through the creation of perfect institutions contained an important psychological insight: that human behavior is, at least partially, a product of social causes. According to the nineteenth-century founders of the new institutions, the cure for crime and mental illness was to separate the individual from the bad company and urban corruption that caused his behavior, and to expose him to the healthful influences of the countryside, the Bible, and hard work. This theory was more accurate about the causes of crime and mental illness than about their cure, as we will argue at the end of the chapter after a look at the performance of the institutions bred by this theory.

A substantial part of this chapter is devoted to a discussion of the concept of the *total institution,* an idea borrowed from sociology and useful, as we will see, in pointing out underlying psychological similarities among the otherwise diverse establishments under investigation. Our central argument is that such institutions create psychological conditions that counteract the positive goals of the institutions. In surveying some of the major facts about social structure and psychological atmosphere in total institutions, we lean heavily on the account provided by Erving Goffman (1961), a student of social establishments with a sharp eye for their human consequences. His characterization of the total institution provides us with a general framework that can be applied to specific discussions of prisons and asylums. The reader should be aware at the outset, however, that the concept of total institution is an abstraction, an "ideal type." No one real institution will conform perfectly to the general description, and every real institution will incorporate many significant phenomena not covered by it.

WORLDS WITHIN WALLS: THE TOTAL INSTITUTION

In Goffman's words, "A total institution may be defined as a place of residence and work where a large number of like-situated individuals, cut off from the wider society for an appreciable period of time, lead an enclosed, formally administered round of life" (Goffman, 1961, p. xii). This definition applies to convents and monasteries, to ships at sea, to boot camps and concentration camps, to some orphanages, boarding schools and old-age homes, and to many other institutions. In our society, the establishments to which it most clearly and significantly applies are mental hospitals and prisons. Frequently, producing some form of change in the individual is a primary purpose of the total institution, though this is not invariably the case.

What is "total" about a total institution? The answer, as Goffman (1961, pp. 5–12) has argued, lies in the attempt of the institution to encompass and regulate almost every aspect of the lives of the individual inmates. All the inmate's activities—eating, sleeping, working, playing—take place in the same physical setting and in the company of more or less the same people, the same cohort of fellow inmates, the same supervisory staff. (The terms "staff" and "inmates" are used loosely here to denote those people who regulate and those who are regulated, respectively. In the case of asylums and prisons these terms may be the ones actually used by the staff. Inmates are likely to use less neutral labels—"hacks," "screws," and more colorful appellations.) Thus, the central social fact of the total institution is the division between staff and inmates, with the former group having, at least officially, an extraordinary amount of power over the latter. Let us now examine the nature and psychological consequences of this division in more detail, concentrating first on the perspective of the staff, and then that of the inmates.

The Psychological World of the Staff

It is a general feature of total institutions that their management procedures stress maintenance of order rather than other institutional goals, and this is true of prisons and asylums despite their avowed purposes of curing the mentally ill and reforming the convicted offender. Ultimately, to understand why this is so, we will have to look outside the walls, at public expectations and public pressures on institutional administrators. However, many of the forces for regimentation arise from the internal dynamics of the institutions themselves. Nowhere are these forces more apparent than in the perspective of the lower-level staff.

Institutional Pressures for Control The situation of lower-level staff in most institutions is not an enviable one. Prison guards and mental hospital attendants are poorly paid and generally receive only a modest amount of training (often just a few weeks) for their work. Moreover, they have little or no hope of promotion to higher positions, for those positions are often reserved for people with years of formal education and specific training. (This is especially true of mental hospitals, where upper-level staff are usually physicians.) Because of their own limited training and low status, as well as the complexity of the institution, staff usually have to operate within a framework of bureaucratic rules that give them very little latitude. They have narrowly defined tasks; they are not free to take much responsibility for working independently with inmates, and at the same time they stand to be censured, or even lose their jobs, if inmates under their supervision deviate too often or too far from the institution's rules. Thus, the staff member's position in a bureaucratic structure breeds some degree of rigidity or impersonality in his relations with inmates, regardless of his own inclinations.

Another factor that reinforces the tendency toward rigidity is the pressure of sheer numbers. The total population of a state prison or mental hospital is commonly in the thousands. At the time of the Attica uprising, for example, that institution held 2,254 men; at any time, between 50 and 100 guards might be on duty, a ratio as high as 45 to 1. Numbers like these make a certain amount of regimentation necessary. For example, it is all but impossible to organize the feeding of large blocs of people unless the organizer can count on groups of known size being in place and ready to eat at prearranged times. This, of course, means that someone must dictate dining hours for inmates. Because the institution regulates not only feeding but almost every other aspect of inmate affairs, rules and scheduling naturally grow complex and minutely detailed. In the past the problems imposed by numbers were exacerbated by chronic overcrowding, especially in state institutions. In recent years, overcrowding has been eliminated in some cases although it persists in others.

Moreover, beyond the external pressures of rules and numbers, subtler internal forces feed the willingness of staff to deal with inmates in impersonal ways. Perhaps the most important of these factors, in prison and mental hospitals, is the tendency of staff to share the negative views of the rest of society regarding the people in their charge. Prison inmates are thought of as criminals. The word does not merely denote the fact that inmates have been found guilty of specific infractions; it inescapably connotes a general moral deficiency, a sense of basic evil and untrustworthiness. Mental patients are perceived as ill or crazy. The strong presumption is that they can be expected to do the irrational and unpredictable. These expectations, of course, are periodically confirmed: riots and escape attempts occur in prison; mental patients do engage in violent outbursts. The point is not that such expectations are without foundation, but that they tend to be applied indiscriminately to all inmates. Goffman points out that there is little the individual inmate can do to escape such stereotypes; his presence in the institution is taken as proof that they apply. Personal contact between individual staff and inmates may erode such stereotypes in particular cases, but they are hard to escape entirely.

The Means and Limits of Control So far we have considered the staff's focus on the goal of order, and the way in which that goal is rooted in the staff's conception of inmates and in the structure of the institution. It remains for us to discuss the means available to staff for implementing their goal. Control in any social organization depends in part on what behavioral psychologists call systems of reinforcement—rewards meted out so as to make some kinds of behavior more likely, and punishments levied so as to reduce the probability of other kinds of behavior. The reinforcers available to staff for controlling inmate behavior are crucial in the overall functioning of the institution, and grow out of its basic social structure.

Because inmates have few rights, and the most elementary freedoms are seen as privileges, the staff's power to grant or withhold such privileges can be used selectively to reward desired behavior and punish unwanted behavior. In an atmosphere of pervasive regulation and deprivation of autonomy, seemingly minor matters (a little extra privacy, permission to walk on the grounds, or use the recreation rooms, etc.) can be effective reinforcers. Officially, control in these matters may be the prerogative of upper staff—wardens, psychiatrists, and the like. However, lower staff often control the inmate's official image through formal reports on inmate behavior or informal discussion with superiors. The doctor, counselor, or administrator, operating under the pressure of case overloads and barely familiar with the inmate, often has little choice but to rely on the nonprofessional judgments of those who deal with the inmate daily. An inmate represented as a malcontent may get from upper staff a response very different from one depicted by lower staff as serious in his efforts at cure or reform.

A final crude class of aversive reinforcers is use of physical restraints and corporal punishment. Confinement ("solitary" in prison, restraining garments and locked cells in mental hospitals) is usually the most extreme form of punishment legally available to staff. Beatings and other physical mistreatment, while never officially permitted, undoubtedly occur, if there is any truth at all to the frequent allegations of ex-prisoners and mental patients (and the occasional admission of administrators). Physical punishment is a more sensitive issue in prisons than asylums (although see the discussion of shock therapy below) and it is in penitentiaries that the most drastic examples occur, for inmates can "legitimately" be killed under extreme circumstances.

In viewing the regulatory systems of prisons and asylums through the lens of behavioral psychology, we have spoken of systems of reinforcement and behavior control; however, staff themselves would use very different terminology. In staff language, privileges are extended because "the patient's illness appears to be in remission." Patients are placed in restraint "for their own safety." Even in prisons, where issues of control are faced more squarely, the recalcitrant is disciplined "so that he will learn to be a law-abiding citizen in the institution as well as outside." Behavior control is justified in terms of personal change in the inmate, not in terms of the staff's convenience or the institution's smooth functioning.

The point is not that the staff's characterizations are invariably hypocritical, but rather that the same actions may be viewed in different lights. Particularly important examples are the use of shock therapy and drugs in mental hospitals. Many physicians view shock as a legitimate form of therapy, effective in dealing with cases of depression. However, many patients find the experience extremely unpleasant (although painless) and regard it as a form of physical punishment. This was especially true in the past, when shock was indiscriminately used for a wide variety of symptoms. In some cases its use as punishment was quite blatant (see Belknap, 1956, p. 192). Similarly, drugs produce dramatic improvement in some manifestations of mental disorder; they too can be regarded both as therapeutic tools and as a means of behavior control. Of course, there are many cases in which patients accept, or actively seek, drug and shock therapy.

All that has been said may leave the reader with the impression that the staff of the total institution is practically omnipotent with respect to inmates. This, however, is far from the truth; the power of the staff is undercut by several factors. These have been outlined by Gresham Sykes (1958, Chap. 3), in a discussion of prisons that applies to other institutions as well.

First, Sykes points out that the rewards and punishments available to prison staffs are inadequate. The inmate has already been deprived of liberty, property, the company of his friends and family, heterosexual contact, meaningful work, and satisfying recreation. Although petty reinforcements acquire disproportionate importance in institutional situations, the fact is that the punishments that can *legally* be added to the inmate's burden are *relatively* minor. (Physical punishment, of course, is another matter. It is illegal, but it occurs precisely because other punishments are so ineffective.)

In the sphere of rewards, the staff has even less to offer. Many important privileges within the walls—mail, visitors, recreational privileges—are given the inmate as a right. They may be stripped from him as punishment, but they cannot be dangled before him as rewards. In prisons, even "good time"—the time deducted from the inmate's sentence for good behavior—is given him in a block at the time of entry, and then chipped away as he commits infractions within the walls. In short, even potential rewards are turned into punishments. This is somewhat less true of mental hospitals, where privileges are extended as the patient shows signs of improvement. Even in mental hospitals, however, threats of punishment—loss of privileges, assignment to a locked ward—are used at least as much as systematic positive reinforcement. The only really significant reward contingent on the inmate's behavior, i.e., release from the hospital or parole from prison, is far removed from everyday interaction and has an all-or-nothing quality that makes it ineffective for shaping specific behavior. Moreover, it too is likely to be turned into a threat, that is, refusal of discharge.

This bias toward punishment is important because, even in animal experiments, punishment is not as effective as positive reinforcement in sustaining behavior patterns over long periods. Animals trained by punitive techniques tend to lapse into their old behavior patterns as soon as the punishing agent is absent. Also, they tend to develop aggressive or neurotic behavior, and to try to escape the situation entirely. Humans exposed to the punitive atmosphere of total institutions show remarkably similar reactions.

A second factor limiting the power of the staff over inmates is the fact that inmates have some power to reinforce staff behavior. If a guard or an attendant is excessively strict, his charges can retaliate by being noisy, disorderly, and otherwise breaking minor rules. This gives the staff member a bad reputation with his superiors because it appears that he can't handle inmates. Therefore, staff find it expedient to ignore some rules so they can enforce others.

A third limiting factor is the "corruption" of the attendant or guard by ordinary face-to-face dealings with inmates. The desire to be seen as a "good guy" and to interact smoothly with others is a barrier to strict enforcement of rules. This general predilection is reinforced by the fact that lower staff and inmates are in some respects in a similar situation: both are subject to the role of higher administrators, and both share many of the same complaints about petty details of institutional procedure. Moreover, lower staff and inmates often share roughly the same social class and educational background, and thus have more in common with one another than either group does with higher administrators.

Perhaps the most important limitation on the power of the staff arises from a very general psychological principle: no institution, and no society, can pin its hopes for stability and smooth functioning entirely on external behavioral controls of the type we have discussed. Social psychologist Herbert Kelman (1961) has called this type of influence (which is so dependent on tangible rewards and punishments) "compliance." He points out that compliance is dependent on surveillance: in the case of institutions, surveillance entails the ability of the staff to monitor the behavior of individual inmates and apply reinforcement at appropriate times. However, even in the tightly controlled world of the total institution, surveillance is imperfect. Inmates will often escape punishment for prohibited behavior, and, as we will see, other inmates may impose a system of reinforcements which counters that of the staff. Truly effective social control requires that the governed individual accept the authority of his governors as a personal or moral imperative. In Kelman's terminology, he must accept the rules imposed on him either because of *identification* (a desire to maintain a positive relationship with those in authority) or because of *internalization* (a recognition that the rules accord with his own values or motives). Needless to say, this essential state of affairs is not invariably achieved in total institutions. In Gresham Sykes' analogy, the inmate "society of captives" is like a conquered province, grudging in its partial acceptance of staff authority and, in prisons at least, ready for rebellion under the right circumstances.

All the factors just outlined, together with the excessive rigidity of institutional rules, guarantee that the rules cannot be fully enforced. The nominal power of the staff is very great; its actual power may be much less. Even with prolonged personal contact and the cooperation of the patient, fully trained psychotherapists may fail to help mental patients, and no one has a formula for reforming criminals. It is not surprising, then, that lower staff in total institutions, constrained by rules, faced with responsibility for supervising large numbers of people, yet limited in actual power, can do little but act as custodians. Ordinary flexibility in personal relations is all but impossible, let alone serious efforts at cure or reform.

The Psychological World of the Inmates

So far we have concentrated on the staff side of the inmate-staff cleavage, spelling out some of the influences on the staff that explain why they treat inmates as they do. Let us now look at the institution from the inmates' point of view. How do inmates respond, collectively and individually, to the treatment they receive?

Collective Responses: The Inmate Culture No matter how close the surveillance of the staff, no matter how severe the punishments for violations of the rules, a kind of inmate counterculture seems to be a nearly universal feature of total institutions. How elaborate the inmate society is depends on the circumstances of the institution: on back wards for chronic psychotic patients, who interact with each other minimally if at all, a subculture could hardly be said to exist. Under most conditions, however, interaction among inmates is more lively; inmates construct their own patterns of authority, codes of behavior, and views of the world, and the institution. Often these views and codes are opposed to those of the staff. In prisons, inmate society reaches its height of complexity and opposition to the institution.

Like the staff, the inmate culture uses a variety of reinforcers to control the behavior of its members. Some, notably physical coercion and material inducements, are similar to those employed by staff (although, of course, their use by inmates is covert and illicit). Particularly in prisons, physical intimidation is relatively common, as is exchange of contraband goods such as food, clothing, pinups and pornography, drugs, and makeshift weapons. In American penal institutions cigarettes function as a kind of money; they are traded, hoarded, gambled for, and used to pay for goods and services of various kinds. Homosexual activities also enter the exchange system of the prison; they may be offered in trade for contraband, or for physical protection, or in order to avoid a beating.

Inmate exchange systems can be seen as part of a broader system of behavior control that tends to maintain the inmate subculture. Indeed, some social psychologists have tried to analyze all human interaction as a series of exchanges, in which one man's behavior is another man's reward, and vice versa. A recent treatment is Kenneth Gergen's *The Psychology of Behavior Exchange* (1969). Gergen observes that in systems of social exchange the most general, and in many cases the most powerful, reinforcers are acceptance and approval, and the most effective punishments are ostracism and rejection. These facts have special importance in the context of the total institution, for approval is the main reinforcer in the arsenal of the inmate culture. In institutional settings the impact of approval by fellow inmates is augmented by the absence of alternative peer groups. Outside the walls, one can usually locate a subculture or a set of friends that approves of behavior the rest of society labels deviant (witness communities of drug users or homosexuals). Such choices of associates are likely to be drastically limited in the confines of an institution.

An important related function of the inmate culture is to offer the inmate a definition of self and situation that can serve as an alternative to the one being forced on the new inmate by the staff. In prisons and asylums alike, it is usually bad form to ask another inmate "what he's in for." And, when another inmate offers an explanation for his presence in the institution, one doesn't question it, even if it is an obvious distortion. Collective acceptance of his "story" allows the inmate to save face in a humiliating situation.

Despite what has been said so far it would be an error to exaggerate the power of the inmate culture relative to that of the institution. Much of the power wielded by inmates depends on the acquiescence or active collaboration of the staff, and can be taken away by the staff. For example, an inmate may acquire leverage in the inmate society through his institutional job. An extreme case was Stanley Randall, a con man serving an eleven-year sentence in Philadelphia's Holmesburg Prison. Randall was employed as an assistant in a research project conducted in the prison by the University of Pennsylvania; his job gave him the power to decide which inmates would serve as subjects in various tests. Inmates were paid as much as $100 for participating—a fortune in the prison economy. Thus, Randall's power was enormous, and he used it to secure sexual favors from other prisoners in return for "getting them on the tests" (Davis, 1971).

When the staff of a total institution understands the function of the inmate subculture, it can actually exploit that subculture to its own ends. A striking example was the treatment of American prisoners by the Communist Chinese during the Korean War (Schein, 1956). The Chinese carefully separated officers from enlisted men and elevated the least prestigious members of captured units to positions of influence, in an attempt to replace existing lines of authority with new ones engineered by the captors. In Korea and in China itself after the 1949 revolution (Lifton, 1961) programs of "thought reform" made extensive use of "progressive" (i.e., cooperative) inmates to exert pressure on new men. Thus thought reform incorporated an explicit effort to shape the inmate culture so as to serve the institution's purposes.

It would also be a mistake to exaggerate the degree of solidarity involved in inmate cultures. As Gresham Sykes (1958) points out, the inmate society has "alienative" as well as "cohesive" tendencies: on the one hand, it draws inmates together, causing them to share some common standards and beliefs (the cohesive tendency); on the other hand, as the example of Stanley Randall makes dramatically clear, it furnishes opportunities for single inmates to build up private islands of power and privilege, often at the expense of other inmates (the alienative tendency). Social divisions carried over from the outside world—race being the prime example—also tend to pit inmates against one another. Therefore, while small groups or pairs of inmates ("cliques" or "buddies" in Goffman's terms) may show intense loyalty, inmate organizations that are both tightly knit and broadly based rarely exist for any length of time. Concerted action of the type that took place at Attica does occur periodically, but it is generally short-lived.

These internal divisions of the inmate society account for the somewhat paradoxical fact that inmate *codes* are described by inmates as universally accepted prescriptions for behavior, but are commonly violated in reality. For example, in both prisons and asylums there almost invariably exists a strict prohibition against reporting another inmate's "illegal" activities to the staff. There is also almost invariably a network of informers who guarantee that any activity widely known to inmates will also become known to staff.

Inmate cultures, then, tend to be loosely structured. They do not offer the individual a single comprehensive alternative to the world imposed by the staff. What they offer at best is a set of possibilities, open to different inmates in varying degrees, which make the regimen of the institution a little more bearable. What they offer at worst is a set of additional pressures, equally unbearable. The floating libraries of illegal books that often circulate around prisons are examples of inmate social arrangements of the first kind. The homosexual assaults rife in some jails are extreme examples of the second.

Individual Responses The individual inmate of a total institution lives in three social worlds at once. Two of these have been discussed: the world of the institution and its staff and the world of the inmate culture. The third is the larger world outside, which can never be totally excluded from the institution. Usually it intrudes in the concrete form of personal visits from relatives and friends, newspapers, magazines, and television. Even where these amenities are absent, it is present in the memories of inmates and staff. Since social environments are never inert, but always exert active influence upon the individual, the three worlds of the inmate subject him to three sources of pressure, often in conflict with one another. He must try to find a way to behave that is consonant with the values and self-concept which he brings to the institution from outside but which also allows him to coexist peacefully with the staff and other inmates.

Goffman suggests that inmates choose some mixture of four basic responses to the pressures of the institution (1961, pp. 61-65):

1 *The intransigent line.* The inmate may resist all attempts by the institution to control his behavior and attitudes. He "intentionally challenges the institution by flagrantly refusing to cooperate with the staff." This is the stuff of which movies about heroic prisoners-of-war are made, but in reality it is usually a temporary stage the inmate goes through when he arrives. The pressures of the institution are too strong to allow many to hold the intransigent line for long; most find it expedient sooner or later to slide toward one of the other response patterns. It is important to realize that when the intransigent inmate defies the staff over some trivial rule, he is not just being selfish or perverse; he is trying to retain his view of himself as an autonomous person who makes choices that affect his life. The intransigent inmate is one who rejects identification with either staff or fellow inmates, and tries to hold onto old loyalties and values by brute force. Because he makes life stressful for everyone around him, the "ball buster," as intransigent inmates are called in prison argot, is not likely to be a hero to his fellow inmates, who have made other accommodations to the institution.

2 *Situational withdrawal.* The inmate may try to ignore the life of the institution, concentrating his attention only on what immediately affects him. Such an inmate interacts as little as possible with other inmates and staff. Like intransigence, withdrawal protects the inmate from the encroachment of the institution. Goffman speaks of withdrawal as a kind of stupor; his examples are "regression" in mental hospitals and "prison psychosis" in penitentiaries. There are more active and positive kinds of withdrawal, however. Bruno Bettelheim (1943), for example, reports how he used the techniques to retain his integrity in a Nazi concentration camp: he clung to his profession as a psychologist, adopting the attitude of a participant observer in the camp, studying its effects on inmates. The result was that he, unlike other prisoners, never lost his sense of relationship with the outside world, and he eventually produced widely read books and articles about his experience.

3 *Colonization.* The inmate may accept the institution as his world and try to build a satisfactory life within its limits. The world outside ceases to be something he longs for, and against which he compares his life inside. The colonized inmate identifies primarily with the inmate culture and internalizes its values. He finds security and a measure of happiness within the walls.

Since inmate codes rarely permit him to see any virtues in the institution, and since staff too may be embarrassed by inmates who seem to see the institution as a "soft deal," the colonized inmate may mask his satisfaction under the usual complaints. The colonized attitude comes to the surface, however, when discharge is imminent. A well-known phenomenon in both prisons and asylums is "messing up," a last-minute infraction of the rules or reappearance of symptoms that postpones the inmate's release.

4 *Conversion.* The inmate may accept the viewpoint of the staff and the institution, striving to be a model prisoner or patient. The convert differs from the colonized inmate in that the latter merely tries to make the best of life within the institution; he may remain quite cynical

about the institution's avowed goals, the conduct of the staff, and the view of himself held by the institution and staff. In contrast, the convert adopts the institutional rationales, i.e., the staff's explanation for their behavior and the official picture of himself as well. He internalizes the values of the institution, and, so far as possible, identifies with the staff.

Most inmates work out a personal stance toward the institution that combines elements of all four basic strategies in varying degrees. As Goffman says, the typical mix is best characterized as "playing it cool" —the strategy of the inmate who tries to "pull his time" as pleasantly as possible, to avoid trouble and to get himself out.

None of the four modes of adaptation to the institution is likely to serve the goals of cure or reform. Intransigence and some forms of withdrawal are attempts to circumvent the pressures of the institution altogether, and to hold on to a former life-style. Colonization turns the inmates away from the outside world, toward a permanent life in the institution. Conversion *might,* under ideal circumstances, be a positive force, but only where the staff is genuinely engaged in trying to return inmates to a productive life outside the walls. Since institutional pressures make such an orientation rare, conversion is likely to work much like colonization.

Total Institutions as Agents of Change

Our review of the characteristics of total institutions leads us to one major conclusion: the segregation of the inmate from society, together with the bureaucratic regimentation of his life within the walls, causes him to focus his attention and energy on adapting to the institution. His adaptation may take many forms, but almost none of its forms is likely to make him a healthier, happier, more moral, or more productive citizen of the world outside the walls. The inmate may have positive experiences in the institution—school, vocational training, contact with an able psychotherapist, attendant, or prison guard. He may change for the better as a result. However, the institution itself does little to strengthen or facilitate such change. At best it functions as a neutral setting for positive experiences; more typically, it undercuts and obstructs them.

Critics of mental hospitals and prisons sometimes suggest that the fault in those systems lies with the quality of the staff. If only "better people" could be attracted into mental health and corrections work, e.g., by higher salaries, conditions would improve, it is said. Other critics adopt quite the opposite perspective; they argue that attempts at cure and reform are misguided and wasteful, since mental patients are hopelessly sick and convicts hopelessly stubborn. Our investigation of the characteristics of total institutions suggests that both sets of critics may be wrong. The institutional pressures we have outlined would tend to frustrate the efforts even of able staff and cooperative inmates. Reform must come from an understanding of the structural inadequacies of institutions and the relation of institutions to society.

In the following sections we turn to a specific examination of prisons and mental hospitals, using as a framework three general questions:

1 What changes is the institution intended to produce? (And what implicit or explicit psychological assumptions govern the way the institution is organized to achieve these goals?)

2 What *actual* changes do the institutions produce? (And how can psychology help examine them?)

3 How is the institution responding to the discrepancy between intended and actual results? (And what role is psychology playing in those reforms?)

PRISONS

The prison system in the United States is a tangled web of city, town, and county jails, state reform schools, penal farms and work camps, and state and federal penitentiaries. It is difficult to specify their populations precisely because inmates come and go from local jails so frequently; however, during the mid-sixties it was estimated that over two million Americans spent time in some form of jail each year and that about 250,000 adult males were residing in federal and state prisons (Glaser, 1964, p. 11). Ninety-seven percent of inmates are men; a majority are black, Puerto Rican, Mexican-American, and Indian (Geller, 1972).

Convicted inmates of town and municipal jails are usually serving sentences for misdemeanors such as drunkenness, disturbing the peace, etc. However, it is one of the scandals of our criminal justice system that many inmates of such institutions have never been convicted of any crimes; they are accused persons awaiting trial and too poor to raise bail money. In New York City, more than 70 percent of all jail inmates are in this category. Because of congestion in the courts, such people may spend many months in jail before being brought to trial. (Usually the pretrial term in jail is deducted from the sentence—*if* sentence is passed.)

Inmates of state and federal penitentiaries are almost invariably convicted felons. Crimes against property (burglary, robbery, fraud, embezzlement, etc.) account for most of the convictions. Violent crimes against the person (murder, rape, manslaughter, assault) make up most of the rest. It should be noted, however, that many inmates are convicted of crimes considerably less serious than those of which they were originally accused. This occurs because plea bargaining has become common practice in the courts: the accused person pleads guilty to a lesser crime, receiving a lesser sentence, and sparing judges, lawyers, and the state, a time-consuming, costly trial. This practice has been widely attacked because it allows the guilty to avoid just punishment, while encouraging the innocent to plead guilty to relatively minor crimes in order to avoid the risk of a long sentence.

Much could be written about what precedes the convict's arrival at the prison—about the functions of the police, about the inequities of the legal and judicial system, most of all about the social roots of crime. Although our concern here is with the period during and after imprisonment, the reader should keep in mind the fact that the prison does not exert its influence on the inmate in isolation; for him imprisonment is just one part of his total experience with the law enforcement and criminal justice system.

What Changes Do Prisons Try to Produce?

In the words of a prison sociologist, society expects prisons to perform at least four functions: "incapacitation, retribution, deterrence and reformation" (Donald Cressey, quoted in Goffman, 1961, p. 83).

The first two goals are achieved by custody itself. Incapacitation —temporary prevention of further harm to society by the offender —is achieved by segregating him from normal life. Retribution, the infliction of psychological pain or inconvenience as punishment for misdeeds, likewise is accomplished through the inmate's loss of freedom.

Officially, at least, no further pains (e.g., the isolation, backbreaking labor, or bread-and-water diets of former years) are deemed necessary or appropriate, except as punishment for further infractions within the walls.

Achievement of the second two goals is more problematic. Deterrence and reformation require psychological change in the individual; deterrence refers to the reduced likelihood of further crime on the part of the inmate, and of others who might be moved to commit crimes, brought about by the threat of punishment. Reform implies some kind of positive change in the inmate, an improvement in his moral values, self-restraint, or capacity to function in a socially useful role. Neither of these changes is an automatic consequence of imprisonment. In order for deterrence to occur, the pains of imprisonment must be salient to the individual at the moment he contemplates a crime and must outweigh the possible gains of criminal activity. In order for reform to occur, the prison experience must include positive elements that somehow offset the negative effects of the institutional environment.

A key point concerning these four goals is that they easily lead to conflicting policies. In particular, strict regimentation may make the prison more secure against escape and inmate misbehavior, but it may also embitter the inmate and interfere with constructive activities (as, for example, when inmates in a job training program are denied the use of essential tools that might be used to make weapons). Correction officials frequently point out that regimentation and reform are not inevitably and entirely in conflict: indeed, it is hard to see how any program of vocational training, counseling, or whatever could succeed except in an atmosphere of order and security. When the inmate is subjected to bullying by his peers, when he is surrounded by the attractions of contraband goods and services, he is unlikely to be much impressed by the authority of the institution or its attempts to change his behavior. Moreover, the experience of order itself may be a force for reform; by being compelled to curb deviant behavior inside the walls, the inmate may become a little more likely to curb it outside. Unfortunately, arguments like these can become rationalizations for regimentation far beyond what is required to serve the goal of reform.

In view of the difficulty of achieving the goals of deterrence and reform, and in view of the institutional pressures toward order and regimentation discussed earlier, it is not surprising that maintenance of custody and order is seen by most prison administrators as essential, whereas rehabilitation is seen as merely desirable. To these forces may be added another, crucial, pressure toward regimentation: society at large exacts a far higher penalty from the staff and administration of the prison when custody is breached than when its efforts at reform fail. An escape or riot can cost a warden his job; the continued release of inmates who go on to commit new crimes may be decried by legislators and the press, but the blame is likely to be placed on the criminal, or "the system," not on the individual administrator.

The emphasis on custody is, however, a shortsighted one from society's point of view. The obvious fact is that almost all prisoners get out (99 percent according to Glaser, 1964, p. 3; Glaser states that 115,000 men are released from state and federal penitentiaries each year). If the convict returns to the streets unchanged, or worse, angry and newly schooled in criminal techniques, society has surely done itself a disservice in encouraging its prison administrators to concentrate on custody rather than reform. The stress on custody and order can be justified only by their presumed deterrent function: if prison does not change men for the better, perhaps at least it scares them into avoiding crime in the future.

What Changes Do Prisons Actually Produce?

With respect to the goal of incapacitation, conceived merely as the prevention of escape, little need be said. Escapes make news, but they are relatively rare. Walls and bars, guards and guns are effective deterrents, made far more effective by the anticipated unpleasantness of life as a fugitive, and by the possibility of parole after a period of time on good behavior. With respect to maintenance of order within the walls, matters are much more complicated. On the one hand, prison routine is followed to a large extent: inmates get up and go to sleep, eat and work on schedule; the buildings and grounds are maintained, the laundry done, the license plates manufactured. On the other hand, infractions of the rules are widespread. Insubordination, fights, gambling, forced and consensual homosexuality are everyday occurrences. This state of affairs can be understood in terms of our earlier discussions concerning the inmate culture and the limitations on the power of the staff.

With respect to the goal of retribution, it is clear that the pains of imprisonment are severe and deeply felt. Gresham Sykes (1958,

Chap. 4) catalogues them as follows: the deprivation of liberty, autonomy, physical security, economic goods and services, and heterosexual contact. The losses of liberty and autonomy have already been discussed in detail in connection with the general features of total institutions. Physical insecurity and sexual and economic deprivation have special relevance for prisons and deserve some elaboration.

In discussing economic deprivation, some observers, noting that many inmates come from backgrounds of poverty, have argued that the food, clothing, and shelter provided by the institution make the inmate better off economically than he would be outside the walls. This is true for some but not for others; moreover, the inmate typically *feels* himself to be deprived, regardless of the objective situation. Wages paid for labor in prison are meager (pennies per hour in most cases), and the inmate is not allowed to spend more than a few dollars per week received from outside. This is done to prevent theft, fights, and gross financial inequalities within the prison, but the psychological effect is to exacerbate the inmate's sense of deprivation. The fact that the inmate personally controls so little money weighs heavily against the fact that necessities are provided.

With respect to physical insecurity, even the toughest street fighters live with some degree of fear in prison, at least during their initial period inside. (See, for example, the autobiographical account of Piri Thomas, 1967.) New inmates share to some degree society's stereotype of their fellows: they expect them to be like animals in a jungle. Experience counters the most unrealistic fears, but some level of anxiety remains. The weak man knows that he may become prey to the "gorilla"; the strong man knows that he may be challenged precisely because of his reputation as a "tough."

In the prison environment, the lack of physical security is exacerbated by the lack of heterosexual contact. The lack of sex itself can be borne, but it creates a situation in which homosexuality becomes prevalent, and this is a basic threat to many men. Much of the homosexual activity in prison takes place by mutual consent. Even consensual homosexuality can entail problems of guilt, especially for men who were heterosexual outside the walls. However, it is forced homosexuality that breeds deep fear on the part of many inmates and that has occupied the attention of prison reformers. Some ex-inmates claim that the extent of homosexual rape has been exaggerated in media accounts of prison life. But reputable investigators have found it to be prevalent to a horrifying degree in some correctional systems. For example, a Philadelphia Assistant District Attorney, commissioned by a municipal judge to investigate the problem, estimated that nearly 2,000 sexual assaults took place in three Philadelphia jails during a two-year period (Davis, 1971).

The goals of reform and deterrence are considerably harder to assess, just as they are harder to achieve. One commonly accepted, though indirect and inadequate, measure of the effectiveness of deterrence and reform is the *recidivism rate*, the proportion of released inmates who are convicted of new crimes or parole violations and returned to prison. Presumably, the lower the recidivism rate, the more successful the penal system. Since the 1940s, it has been a tenet of popular folklore that the recidivism rate is about two-thirds. This figure, very possibly incorrect, is usually arrived at by surveying the inmate population at a state or federal prison and determining how many inmates are first-timers and how many have prior convictions. Typically, only about a third are serving their first sentence; hence the assumption that two-thirds of those released will be reimprisoned. But the logic is faulty: the fact that two-thirds of those *in* prison *have* committed earlier crimes does not prove that two-thirds of those released *will* commit new crimes. First-timers are usually given shorter sentences than repeaters; therefore the proportion of first-timers *in* prison does not reflect the proportion of *incarcerations* that are *first-time incarcerations.*

What, then, is the recidivism rate? The only way to know is to follow a sample of released prisoners from a wide variety of institutions and see how many return to jail as the years pass. This kind of research is difficult, expensive, time-consuming, and, not surprisingly, rare. One compendium of this kind of data appears in a study conducted by Daniel Glaser (1964). Surveying both his own carefully collected data on federal prison releasees and a variety of other studies, mostly of state institutions, Glaser concludes that the true recidivism rate, overall, is about one-third. About a quarter are new felony convictions, the rest parole violations. (Depending on the parole supervisor and system, parole violations may be serious, e.g., weapons charges, or "technical," e.g., drinking, living with a woman not one's wife, etc.—that is, they may be violations that are not ordinarily considered crimes.) Is this a high or low rate? That, of course, is a judgment the reader must make for himself. Clearly, there is still room for improvement, particularly in view of the likelihood that some released inmates commit new crimes for which they are not caught and convicted. It should also be noted that other studies of recidivism have reported rates close to the traditional two-thirds figure.

It would be an error to conclude from Glaser's data that prisons reform two-thirds of their inmates. Two-thirds may stay out of jail, but no one knows whether this proportion would have been higher, lower, or the same if the criminal had not experienced prison. The problem is analogous to that described in Chapter 2 in connection with psychotherapy. The only way to find out whether prison helps, hurts, or does nothing is to identify a group of convicted but nonincarcerated criminals, similar in backgrounds, personal characteristics, and types of offenses to a group sent to prison, and to see how many new crimes both groups commit over time. Such a comparison is very difficult to make, since men placed on probation, rather than sent to prison, almost always differ in significant ways from those who are sentenced.

In a widely quoted study of this type, conducted in California, groups of first offenders were randomly assigned to prison or to a community treatment program. It was found that 61 percent of those incarcerated and only 38 percent of those in the community program had been convicted of new crimes after a two-year period. Though the data seem to speak strongly against incarceration and for community treatment, they may not be entirely representative; serious offenders had been screened out of the study from the start; the sample consisted mostly of whites; the community program was far more intensive than may be practical on a large scale; and technical parole violations among those in the community group might have been ignored (Wilson, 1973).

In the absence of truly definitive data, we can make only educated guesses about the effectiveness of prisons at deterrence and reform, aided by psychological principles and some of the information available concerning recidivism among different types of releasees.

Glaser (1964, Chap. 3) outlines some characteristics of high-risk releasees and release situations: the younger a man is when first convicted, and the younger he is when released on his present offense, the more likely he is to return to jail. The more prior criminal offenses on his record, the more likely he is to return. The younger he was when he first left home, the more likely he is to be convicted of a new crime.

If he is released to a community with a high crime rate, he is more likely to be jailed again. The relation between recidivism and type of offense is particularly revealing: economic crimes, especially offenses not involving violence (auto theft, forgery, burglary, etc.), have a high recidivism rate; assault, rape, and murder combined have a recidivism rate of 18 percent. Other offenses lie between these extremes.

Conclusions based on such scattered facts cannot be very conclusive; however, the rather large differences in recidivism rates associated with factors not under the prison's control (age, type of crime, etc.), and the stability of these relationships across different institutions, suggest that factors in the offender's social world outside the walls influence him far more than his experience in the institution.

Low-recidivism crimes are situational crimes, murder being an example. Statistically, the "typical" murder is one in which a man kills a member of his family or a close friend in a fit of rage. A crime like this is not likely to be repeated, even if the offender does not suffer the pain of prison. (Of course, the threat of prison *may* add to the self-restraint of former prisoners and people in general, but the nature of the crime makes it seem unlikely that prison functions as a psychological deterrent at the crucial moment. Whether moved by spontaneous passion, as in the case of murder, or by inner compulsion, as in the case of sex crimes, the individual is unlikely to weigh the consequences of his act.)

High-recidivism crimes are career crimes, including notably the many varieties of theft. This type of crime begins with economic deprivation. It usually starts early in life and is nurtured by unemployment, absence of family ties, and—crucially—exposure to criminal peers and models. The impact of prison on this kind of crime is ambiguous: on the one hand, it probably acts as a deterrent to any activities that carry a high probability of detection. On the other hand, it exposes the novice to more experienced criminals who can instruct him in the techniques of his trade. Prisons are often described as schools for crime, and there is no reason to doubt that some young and inexperienced inmates emerge as more skillful and determined criminals (although Glaser presents statistics to show that most of the advice older inmates give to younger ones is of the "keep your nose clean" variety). Former U.S. Attorney General Ramsey Clark also points out that some men emerge from prison as new drug addicts (Geller, 1972, p. 25). On balance, prison seems to be accepted as a kind of occupational hazard for the career criminal. "If you can't pull the time, don't pull the crime" is a jailhouse aphorism.

The reasons for the failure of prisons to reform career criminals are not hard to see. Although there are many significant exceptions, most programs of reform within the correctional system fail to offer the inmate a viable alternative to his way of life. Some large-scale programs that masquerade as reform, e.g., prison industries, are in fact designed to serve the needs of the institution, not the inmate. Forbidden by law to compete with private enterprise, prison industries usually involve the inmate in low-skill work with no relevance to the economic world outside. Prison schools typically are dreary, inadequately equipped facilities that serve only a fraction of the inmates. More fundamentally, they attempt to use traditional educational methods and content with a group of men for whom those approaches have failed in the past. Even the prison library is often all but inaccessible to most inmates, and the collection of books is censored. More useful and realistic programs of vocational training are typically confined to a small number of carefully selected inmates. Programs of counseling and psychotherapy are usually small and understaffed.

Even where worthwhile rehabilitative programs exist, the institutional context interferes with their effectiveness. The dehumanizing effects of the total institution are strong forces opposing any positive change. A dramatic demonstration of the degrading effects of institutionalization is provided in a recent experiment conducted by social psychologist Phillip Zimbardo (1972).

Zimbardo's subjects were two dozen carefully screened volunteers who answered the psychologist's advertisement in a Palo Alto (California) newspaper. All male, they were "mature, emotionally stable, normal, intelligent college students from middle-class homes." None had criminal records of any kind. The subjects agreed to participate in a two-week simulation of prison conditions. By the flip of a coin, half were chosen as "guards" and half as "prisoners." The prisoners were picked up at home unexpectedly by city police in a squad car; they were searched, handcuffed, fingerprinted, and booked at the Palo Alto station house, and then taken to Zimbardo's "prison," where they were stripped, deloused, numbered, and put in cells with two other prisoners. The guards worked eight-hour shifts in groups of three. They were allowed to make up their own rules "for maintaining law, order, and respect."

Zimbardo had to discontinue his study after only six days. In that period both prisoners and guards lost all sense of the boundary between their roles and reality. They began to live their parts, and the behavior that emerged was horrifying to the experimenter. About a third of the guards became actively cruel, seeking ways to dominate and torment their prisoners. The rest were "good guys," decent in their dealings with prisoners, but unwilling to take action to stop the sadistic minority. The prisoners became "servile, inhuman robots," concerned only with individual survival and hatred of the guards. Early prisoner solidarity gave way to an attitude of "each man for himself." On one occasion, two inmates refused to give up their blankets in order to get their cellmate out of solitary confinement. Three men had to be released after four days because of such reactions as hysterical crying, severe depression, and disorganization of thought. Others begged to be "paroled" and offered to return their $15-per-day subject's fees, but they returned to their cells without protest when parole was refused.

In sum, the mere establishment of a guard-prisoner relationship brought about dramatic changes in a group of normal people. The severity of the emotional reactions rules out any possibility that subjects were treating the situation as a game. In Zimbardo's words: "In less than a week the experience of imprisonment undid (temporarily) a lifetime of learning; human values were suspended, self-concepts were challenged, and the ugliest, most base side of human nature surfaced" (Zimbardo, 1972, p. 4).

Finally, there is a subtle psychological factor that obstructs any influence prison might exert in the direction of deterrence or reformation. As psychoanalytic theorists emphasize, guilt and defense mechanisms play an important role in human mental life. Even "hardened criminals" often feel some measure of guilt for their crimes, and any such feelings can be intensified by the humbling experience of imprisonment. At the same time, the prisoner is likely to try to suppress his feelings of guilt, to ward off the anxiety associated with guilt, and to erect defenses that allow him to view his behavior in a blame-free light. Thus, it is extremely common to hear inmates claim they were "railroaded" into jail—even while in the same breath admitting guilt for the crime with which they were charged. "Lots of guys have done more and got away with it" is a common refrain—the presumption being that the others were lucky or had smart lawyers. Most important, the oppressive conditions of the prison furnish the prisoner with a defense mechanism rooted in fact: he may come to feel—and very many do—that he has been subjected to excessive and unfair punishment, that society owes *him* a debt rather than the other way around. This state of mind can provide part of the psychological underpinning for further criminal activities after release.

How Are Prisons Changing?

Nothing we have said is news to anyone familiar with corrections in the United States. Most of our arguments have been made repeatedly by critics of the prison system for decades or more. Some of the worst abuses of prisons, such as physical maltreatment of inmates, intolerable sanitary conditions, etc., have been alleviated to some degree. However, the psychological abuses described here persist. As we have seen, the fault at root lies with a public indifferent or vengeful toward prisoners, with legislatures and prison administrations that express the will of that public, and with basic misconceptions built into the system of institutional segregation itself.

Recognizing the inherent contradictions of the system, progressive judges, wardens, and others in the criminal justice field have taken steps to offset some of the problems intrinsic to the total institution. The most obvious step has been to make far more extensive use of probation and parole than in the past. If prisons damage inmates, the logic goes, keep the criminal out of prison, and tied to his family, job, and community as much as possible. As a result, prison populations have declined by 50,000 over the last decade (Geller, 1972). This is one reason why the overcrowding so frequently criticized in the past has ceased to be a problem in some state institutions. (It remains a severe problem in other state prisons, and in big-city jails.) A related step has been the institution of "furloughs" for inmates, for example, programs that allow them to spend a day or several days outside the walls at school, in training programs, or on the job.

Efforts have been made to change staff hiring practices so that guards are men from the same ethnic and social backgrounds as the men they guard. [At Attica, 85 percent of the prisoners were urban blacks, and every guard a rural white (Geller, 1972).]

Though still limited in scope and outreach, programs designed to facilitate reform within the walls have also been spreading. Increasing numbers of prisons have programs of vocational training based on the straightforward assumption that poverty causes crime, especially economic crime with its high recidivism rate, and that a good job will eliminate poverty and reduce the likelihood of future crime. Efforts have also been made to broaden the psychiatric and counseling services available to inmates and to separate those in special need of psychiatric attention from others. Connected to these reforms has been the creation of more diversified prison systems, designed to separate old from young offenders, first-timers from repeaters, high-escape-risk from low-risk inmates, etc. Coupled with more careful diagnosis at the point of entry, such systems are designed to offset the negative effects of criminal models on younger men and to reduce the mistreatment of prisoners by other prisoners.

A variety of attempts have been made to offset the problems faced by the newly released inmate in readjusting to the outside world. Organizations of former inmates have been especially active in this effort, providing advice on how to get jobs, find housing, training, interim financial support, etc. Ex-inmates and other groups have set up "halfway houses," places where the newly released inmate can live in the company of others in the same category until he has reestablished himself.

Hopeful and well intentioned as all these steps are, the reader should not be misled into thinking that the problems of our corrections systems are approaching solution. The problem is not merely that the different programs are for the most part small and scattered. As many of the current generation of prison reformers have argued, tinkering with the organization and staffing of prisons will not transform them into effective means of dealing with intractable social problems. On the one hand, the ethical objection has been raised that total institutions are by their very nature totalitarian, even—perhaps especially—when staff operate on the most benign motives. As one critic phrased this objection, "The desire to help, when coupled with the desire to control, is totalitarian, because the limits that restrain us when we admit that we are punishing are removed" (Greenberg, 1972). The concept of the prison as a therapeutic milieu has, for example, led to the use of "indeterminate sentencing" in the progressive California system. In indeterminate sentencing, a man is sent to prison not for a fixed period determined by his crime, but for an indefinite period which ends when prison authorities judge him ready for release. The result has been to add uncertainty to the list of the pains of imprisonment—and sentences have been longer wherever the system has been implemented (Greenberg, 1972). Beyond such ethical objections, prisons do not attack the problem of crime at its roots; they, like our entire criminal justice system, deal with the individual criminal, and not with the environment that creates him. We will say more on this general problem after we have examined another form of total institution: the mental hospital.

MENTAL HOSPITALS

Ken Kesey's extraordinary novel, *One Flew Over the Cuckoo's Nest*, depicts a confrontation on a mental hospital ward between Big Nurse, the ward administrator, and a rambunctious patient, Randall Patrick McMurphy. McMurphy is actually not mentally ill, but has feigned symptoms in order to get himself transferred from prison to the hospital, on the grossly mistaken assumption that life in the hospital is preferable. The confrontation is seen through the eyes of another patient, Chief Broom, a gigantic Indian who harbors elaborate delusions that the whole world, and the ward in particular, is manipulated by a malevolent Combine, which controls people by installing wires in their brains. He sees the battle on the ward as a struggle between McMurphy (who hasn't been wired yet) and the Combine (personified by Big Nurse). As the struggle unfolds, the reader comes to see the Chief's delusions as a penetrating metaphor for what is actually occurring: clothing her motives and actions in the sanctified language of psychotherapy, Big Nurse systematically dominates and humiliates her patients, rendering them increasingly passive and dependent, decreasingly able to function outside the ward. Group therapy becomes a nightmarish experience in which she pits patients against one another, exploiting every personal revelation not to build understanding, but to erode the patient's self-confidence and dignity and to maintain her grip on the ward. Always in the background lurk the threats of electroshock therapy and lobotomy (a kind of brain surgery) as punishment for the recalcitrant.

Kesey's book is fiction. It can be read purely as an allegory about human freedom and control. But like Chief Broom's delusions, it may be a fiction that penetrates deeply into the reality of some hospital wards. Dramatic evidence for this claim appears in David Rosenhan's paper "On Being Sane in Insane Places" (1973).

Rosenhan and seven other real-life "McMurphies" feigned a psychotic symptom (hearing voices) and had themselves committed to a total of twelve different mental hospitals. The hospitals were diverse, including both private and public institutions, both underfinanced, poorly staffed hospitals and those with relatively lavish funds and large staff. Except for deceiving the hospital personnel about their initial symptoms and, in some cases, about their occupations, the pseudopatients presented accurate information about their own life histories. Once admitted, they feigned no further psychological disturbance and informed the staff that their symptoms had disappeared.

One important question that Rosenhan wanted to answer was simply whether the sanity of the pseudopatients would be detected. The answer was a clear No. All the pseudopatients were admitted without question, and no questions were raised concerning the genuineness of their illness throughout their stay in the hospital—by doctors or nurses. Other patients, however, frequently voiced suspicion: 35 out of a total of 118 patients living on admissions wards with the pseudopatients questioned the investigators or accused them of deception.

How was this possible? How were trained medical staff able to reconcile the "normal" histories and behaviors of the pseudopatients with the apparently inconsistent symptoms reported? By merging what they learned about the patient's life with their preconceptions about the life histories of the mentally ill. For example, one pseudopatient reported close and warm relations with his wife and children, but admitted that he quarreled with his wife and, on rare occasions, spanked his children. The doctor who interviewed him entered the following comment in the patient's medical record:

> Affective stability is absent. His attempts to control emotionality with his wife and children are punctuated by angry outbursts, and, in the case of the children, spanking. (Rosenhan, 1973, p. 253)

Thus, as Erving Goffman has pointed out, the patient's diagnosis tends to control the staff's interpretation of his behavior, rather than the other way around.

Rosenhan argues that such caution on the part of medical personnel is reasonable in the case of physical illness: the consequences to the patient are much more serious if the doctor erroneously pronounces him healthy than if he is erroneously presumed to be sick and kept in a hospital for tests and observation. In the case of mental illness, however, the reverse may be true. Merely to have been labeled a mental patient stigmatizes the individual as dangerous or incompetent—as public reaction to the short-lived vice-presidential candidacy of Senator Thomas Eagleton made poignantly clear.

Rosenhan and his co-workers also kept careful, written records concerning the behavior of doctors, nurses, and attendants. Typically, the staff had their headquarters in an enclosure (called the "cage" by patients) adjacent to a large room where the patients spent their days. Attendants spent 11.3 percent of their time outside this enclosure, including time spent on routine chores as well as time spent dealing with patients. Doctors and nurses emerged so rarely that percentage of time outside the cage could not be calculated. Day nurses emerged an average of 11.5 times per shift, and physicians 6.7 times per day. The pseudopatients attempted to make contact with doctors and nurses by asking a civil and relevant question. (For example, "Excuse me, doctor, but could you tell me when I will be eligible for grounds privileges?") The pseudopatients were flatly ignored on 71 percent of those occasions by doctors and 88 percent by nurses and attendants. Although one might conjecture that patients have access to doctors in a private setting, rather than in the large dayroom, Rosenhan found that the average patient saw psychiatrists, psychologists, residents, and physicians only 6.8 minutes per day throughout his stay, including time spent in admission and discharge interviews, ward meetings with senior staff present, group and individual psychotherapy, and case presentation meetings.

Rosenhan's is the most recent in a long series of studies suggesting that fundamental conflicts exist between the bureaucratic requirements of institutions and the individual needs of patients. We will review other studies in the course of our discussion below. Hospitals of course vary widely in the degree to which they are able to resolve this conflict, and any generalization is subject to many exceptions. We have already discussed psychotherapy in Chapter 2, and we will not go over the same ground again. Our focus here is not on different approaches to treatment but on institutions as a setting for treatment.

What Changes Do Mental Hospitals Try to Produce?

The institutional care of mental patients is a large-scale operation. According to recent estimates, between 500,000 and 600,000 people live in resident treatment centers at any one time; another 750,000 receive care as outpatients. By far the largest portion of resident patients are in publicly supported institutions, mostly state hospitals. About $3.5 billion is spent each year in caring for the mentally ill, not counting the considerable amount spent on training psychiatrists, psychotherapists, psychiatric nurses, and other treatment personnel (Freeman & Giovannoni, 1969). Half the hospital beds in the country are occupied by mental patients, although this is a somewhat misleading figure, since mental patients are hospitalized much longer than other patients—months or years as opposed to weeks. Mental patients account for a little less than 10 percent of hospital *admissions* (Coleman, 1964, p. 263).

As in the case of prisons, the public seems to expect its mental institutions to perform the dual functions of treatment and maintenance of custody. On the one hand, mental illness, as the very phrase suggests, is seen as a disease. It is assumed that there are mental systems, analogous to bodily systems, which are not functioning properly in the "sick" person. Therefore, he is sent to a "hospital" where he is attended by psychiatrists, who are "doctors," and by psychiatric "nurses." If he is fortunate enough to have a disease for which a known treatment exists, he will be cured; if not, his mind may cure itself, as the body often does, or his illness may become chronic, and he will never get well. On the other hand, quite apart from the aptness of this "medical model," the mentally ill person who gets institutionalized is usually someone whose behavior has become a threat, an annoyance, or a burden to himself or others. A person may commit himself, or in some cases be committed, because he is depressed, anxious, or afraid of what he will do to himself or someone else. Even where there is no realistic hope of treatment, institutionalization insures that the patient's behavior will cease to cause harm, embarrassment, or inconvenience. To a much greater degree than is the case with prisons, however, treatment, not custody, is supposed to be the main goal of mental hospitals; there is some justification for the purely custodial function of prisons, but no one likes to think of mental hospitals as dumping grounds for psychological basket cases.

We remind the reader, however, that the goal of treatment, with its associated assumptions about the nature of mental illness, has itself come under attack during the past decades. In Chapter 2 we mentioned theorists such as Thomas Szasz and R. D. Laing, who question the medical model altogether, arguing that mental illness is an arbitrary social label we apply to people whose behavior is inexplicable or deviant by our own lights—including some people whose oddness grows out of special sensitivity or vision. From this perspective, treatment in a mental hospital is nothing but an attempt to change behavior that someone finds inconvenient, just as custody is an attempt to eliminate the inconvenience by hiding the person.

As we saw in Chapter 2, there are uncertainties surrounding psychiatric diagnosis and psychotherapy that lend support to this radical view. However, we cannot postpone action until the weighty ethical and theoretical disputes between advocates of this perspective and more traditional models are ironed out. The fact is that there are people whose eccentricities are not tolerated by society and require the person to be placed under supervision. For now, mental hospitals are the only facilities we have for dealing with such people. To pick an extreme example, an adult who cannot or will not clothe himself, feed himself, or use a toilet would seem to fall into this category. Such cases can be found on most chronic back wards. Of course, it is one thing to argue that there are people who need care (in the sense of both custody and treatment) and others who want it. It is quite another thing to argue that mental hospitals as presently organized and run are a good vehicle for delivering the needed or wanted care.

What Changes Do Mental Hospitals Actually Produce?

One way to evaluate the effectiveness of mental hospitals is to examine the number of patients admitted, released, and readmitted. To do so is, in effect, to ask whether mental hospitals—by their own definitions— cure their patients, and whether the cures are lasting.

Such questions do not have simple yes-or-no answers. The prognosis for release from a mental hospital varies with the patient's initial diagnosis and his length of stay in the hospital, among many other factors. In 1955, according to U.S. Public Health Service statistics (1969), about

63 percent of first admissions to state and county mental hospitals were eventually returned to the community. This represented a marked improvement over the previous decade; the comparable figure for 1946 was 50 percent. There is good reason to believe that the current figure is still higher; one estimate (Coleman, 1964) puts it at 80 percent. However, it should be kept in mind that the release figure is a somewhat inflated estimate of the cure rate, since many of those released are later readmitted. Of the total admissions 52.9 percent are people who have previously been hospitalized (National Clearing House for Mental Health Information, 1971).

Overall release figures typically include short-term patients who enter the hospital briefly for observation or for temporary relief of an acute condition such as a "nervous breakdown." Such patients often leave within a few weeks. Patients who enter the hospital with a diagnosis of some form of psychosis are much less likely to leave quickly. About 24 percent of first admissions are diagnosed as schizophrenic, but schizophrenics make up about 46 percent of the hospital's long-term population. In contrast, although 5–7 percent of first admissions are diagnosed as psychoneurotic, patients in this category constitute only 1 percent of the resident population (Freeman & Giovannoni, 1969, p. 692; Coleman, 1964, p. 269).

The longer a patient stays in the hospital, the less likely he is ever to leave. Today, most patients are discharged within one year (the first-year discharge rate is 90 percent even among schizophrenics, according to research summarized in Coleman, 1964, p. 311). However, a review of studies on length of hospitalization concludes that the schizophrenic hospitalized continuously for two years has only a 6–7 percent chance of being released (Freeman & Giovannoni, 1969, p. 694). The reader should be aware that most of the data just mentioned were gathered before the 1960s; again, there is reason to believe that the picture has changed since that time and is continuing to change.

The low release rates among long-term patients provided much of the impetus for studies of the mental hospital as an institution. Probably the first work of this kind was done by Harry Stack Sullivan in the early 1930s. However, the approach was largely neglected until the 1950s, when a series of detailed case studies appeared (e.g., Belknap, 1956; Stanton & Schwarz, 1954; Caudill, 1958; Greenblatt et al., 1955; Goffman, 1961). Even before that time it was well understood that the inadequate staffing and facilities of large state institutions prevented them from performing more than a custodial function. Some of the institutional studies began to show that the psychiatric hospital could do worse than fail to provide treatment; it could actively harm patients, rendering them less able to function in the outside world. Moreover, such studies made it clear that the negative effects of the institutions could operate even in the best-staffed and best-equipped hospitals.

Ivan Belknap's (1956) investigation of a large southern state hospital was one such study. The institution suffered from the traditionally recognized problems: overcrowding, inadequate funds, pitifully few qualified psychiatrists or psychologists on the staff. Without minimizing the negative impact of these factors on the quality of care, Belknap concluded that the organization of the institution and its relation to the community were at the heart of the problem. He pointed out that, because of size and numbers, the hospital "must be administered in an impersonal fashion with minimum allowances for personal peculiarities on the part of staff, patients, or relatives. Standard operating procedure is necessarily inflexible and administrative routines dominant." He decried the tendency of the community "to dump into the hospital the residual welfare, mentally deficient, and other types of problematic individuals for whom the community does not provide" (Belknap, 1956, pp. 208-209).

Alfred Stanton and Morris Schwartz studied a very different kind of institution: an exclusive, expensive private hospital in which most patients received three to four hours per week of individual psychotherapy. They concluded that the hospital was moderately successful in effecting lasting improvement of mental disorders. However, they also identified many features of the institution that interfered with therapy. For example, when patients were given orders or refused requests without explanation, conflicts over power came to the fore; when patients were treated in an impersonal manner they engaged in exhibitions of "symptoms" in order to get individual attention (Stanton & Schwartz, 1954, Appendices A and H).

Similar observations were made more recently in another small, high-quality hospital specializing in treatment of borderline psychotic patients (Talbot et al., 1964). Talbot et al. point out that the hospital community is one that must be tolerant of deviant behavior. Yet this tolerance, necessary for the therapeutic function of the institution, can have countertherapeutic effects. Patients are drawn into an atmosphere where "deviancy is normal" and "normality is deviant." The atmosphere is one that encourages patients to dwell on and flaunt their symptoms, to lose contact with the concerns of the outside world, and to avoid or conceal constructive activities or changes.

Goffman's *Asylums* (1961), already discussed at length, is the classic example of the institutional study. As we have seen, Goffman pictures the asylum as an institution by its very nature so preoccupied with internal order that it deprives its patients of autonomy and renders them dependent on the institution. Cut off from normal social contacts and preoccupied with the all-encompassing life of the hospital, they become less and less fit to deal with the outside world.

More recent studies have followed Goffman's lead in focusing on the inmate's adaptation to life in the hospital, particularly those experiences that tend to alienate him from life outside. One such study (Shiloh, 1971) was conducted in a large Veterans Administration hospital. After interviewing 560 patients, Shiloh identified two sharply distinct patient types. The first, about 40 percent of his sample, he called "institutionalized," roughly comparable to the type Goffman called "colonized." The institutionalized patients were at home in the hospital, and even feared that Shiloh's interview was some kind of device to "run them out." They were passive, apathetic, inarticulate, and uncooperative in the interview. Most of them were poor, had little formal education, and few family ties or other links to the outside world. The institutionalized patients were unconcerned about the scarcity of therapeutic facilities at the hospital. In fact, they tended to "keep out of the way" of doctors and staff. When asked what they liked about the hospital, they mentioned the material comforts and recreational facilities. Perhaps most telling of all, institutionalized patients, when asked where patients might go if discharged, could think only of other institutions. The second type of patient, whom Shiloh called "noninstitutionalized," did not correspond to any of Goffman's categories. They comprised about 25 percent of the institution's population. (The remaining 35 percent did not fall into any clear classification.) Noninstitutionalized patients were oriented toward the outside world; unlike the institutionalized, they left the hospital on passes as often as possible. They resented the lack of treatment facilities and staff and denied the therapeutic value of many compulsory activities such as work details.

They planned actively for release and thought of home, rather than another institution, as the alternative to the hospital. Shiloh's observations, while corroborating Goffman's analysis in some important respects, also pointed to two conclusions which, though consistent with Goffman, tend to be obscured by Goffman's emphasis on coercive aspects of the institution: (1) a large proportion of patients are able to maintain their personal integrity in the institution and their orientation toward the outside world and (2) those who become colonized or institutionalized tend to perceive their situation as a relatively pleasant one.

The second conclusion is corroborated and greatly extended in a recent provocative book by Braginsky et al. (1969). Like Shiloh, these researchers found that most long-term patients (those who had been in a large state hospital for over two years) appeared to like the hospital more for its comfortable accommodations and recreational facilities than for its therapeutic opportunities (80 percent or more knew the location of the gym, swimming pool, and bowling alley; only 26 percent could name the psychologist or social worker in their own building).

Even more striking was the fact that patients were skilled in "impression management," i.e., using their "symptoms" as a way to get what they wanted from the staff. In an experimental study, long-term patients were brought in for an interview with one of the research psychologists. On the way to the interview, the patient was told the ostensible purpose of the interview by an accomplice of the experimenter posing as attendant. Some patients were told that the purpose was to determine whether the patient belonged on a locked or open ward; others were told that its purpose was to determine whether the patient was ready for discharge from the hospital. Believing that long-term patients actually want to stay in the hospital, but that they want maximum freedom within the institution, the authors predicted that patients would present themselves as "sick" when confronted with the possibility of discharge, and "well" when confronted with the possibility of confinement on a locked ward. (Note that to accomplish this the patient must understand what kinds of behavior will be seen as sick and well by medical staff and to act convincingly on his knowledge.) The expectation was strongly confirmed: when tapes of the interview were played to three psychiatrists, the doctors saw significantly more pathology among the patients "threatened" with discharge than among those threatened with the locked ward. Patients were able to manipulate doctors' judgments to their own ends.

This experiment was only one of nine studies employing a variety of techniques and covering patient behavior in structured experimental situations, in the hospital environment, and outside the hospital. The authors interpreted their research as supporting a radically new view of the patient's relation to the hospital: far from being a passive victim, either of a disease that renders him incompetent in social relations or of an all-controlling, all-encompassing institution, the mental patient is a competent, active human being who controls his environment to suit his own purposes. For many long-term patients especially, the hospital functions as a kind of pleasant, undemanding refuge from the outside world, not as a prison or as a setting for treatment.

What is noteworthy about the findings of Shiloh and Braginsky et al. is that the adaptations of institutionalized patients to the hospital make them less likely ever to leave. They may not be docile victims of oppressive regimentation, but neither are they people in a process of constructive change. Enforced passivity and confinement are not the only ways in which institutions cut people off from the outside world; the pleasures of relief from responsibility—a form of what Sigmund Freud called the "secondary gains" of mental illness—may be a more seductive force.

In summary, our investigation of the changes produced by mental hospitals has led to the following conclusions: most patients are eventually released from mental hospitals and make satisfactory adjustments to life outside. However, studies of the hospital as an institution suggest that, whatever potential value the hospital may have as an environment for change, it is also a milieu fraught with dangers of rendering patients passive, docile, or all too satisfied with their "home."

How Are Mental Hospitals Changing?

Far more than the field of corrections, the fields of psychiatry, clinical psychology, and mental health are in a state of ferment. New ideas are constantly being tried, amended, accepted, or rejected. Most of this experimentation has been done on a small scale, and much of it is confined to private hospitals and therapists in individual practice. Also, much of it is concerned with different approaches in psychotherapy, and, as we have seen, few patients in large public hospitals receive extensive psychotherapy. However, some contemporary changes in the field of mental health grapple with the realities facing the great bulk of patients still in state hospitals. Many important new developments are direct and indirect responses to the shortcomings of institutions as we have pictured them.

Beginning in the early fifties, partly under the impetus of experimental programs conducted in Great Britain, mental health professionals in this country began to think of the hospital as a "therapeutic community" (the title of an influential book by British therapist Maxwell Jones, 1953). This approach recognized the effects of the hospital milieu on the patient, and attempted to involve nurses, attendants, other lower-level staff, and patients themselves in a coordinated effort to bring about positive change. The approach stood in contrast to the traditional view of the doctor as exclusive healer, with other staff expected to perform only custodial functions. In practice, the concept often became no more than a general relaxation of restrictions on patients, though Jones himself had warned against the danger of making the hospital too pleasant a place, and failing to require the patient to readjust to the outside world (Jones, 1953, pp. 159-160). Despite the generally high regard in which the concept of the therapeutic community was and is held, there is evidence that such hospitals, including Jones' own, do not improve the rate of release of patients (Rapoport, 1960).

A more focused approach to treatment in the institution, and one that has shown evidence of success in a variety of studies, is the use of the operant conditioning or behavior modification techniques discussed in Chapter 2. As indicated in that chapter, such techniques are often implemented in the form of token economies, which can be seen as an attempt to use the controlling power of the hospital environment in a positive way.

Many of the new developments in mental health have less to do with improving institutions than with using them as little as possible. Probably the most important change in the hospitals is one that has been underway since 1956 and which has accelerated markedly in the last few years; that change is simply the reduction of the number of people in hospitals, due not to fewer admissions, but to an increasing proportion of releases (Freeman & Giovannoni, 1969, p. 694). In 1968, for example, about 25,000 more people were discharged from mental institutions than were admitted (Statistical Abstracts of the U.S., 1971). State and County mental hospitals cut their resident populations by 24 percent between 1955 and 1967 (U.S. Public Health Service, 1969). Some hospitals have changed little in this regard, while others have cut their resident populations drastically. New techniques of treatment, especially drugs that eliminate the more extreme symptoms of some classes of mental disorder, have made the rapid return of patients to the community practical at a time when therapists have been coming to appreciate its desirability. This policy has the twin advantages of encouraging the patient to readjust to the outside world, while at the same time leaving the hospital free to concentrate its therapeutic resources on the reduced number of remaining patients. The growing numbers of releases are not cures in the traditional sense. Released patients may still suffer from symptoms of various kinds, but they are able to function without full-time supervision. Questions can of course be raised as to whether the released patients are "ready," whether the practice of encouraging release is hazardous to the community. While definitive data are not available, the best rebuttal to this objection is the fact that no one has yet reported drastic increases in either antisocial acts committed by ex-mental patients or in recommitments to mental hospitals.

Along with the increasing frequency of release has come an expansion of facilities for outpatient care and postrelease care. Night hospitals, day hospitals, and outpatient clinics all provide some form of care, but leave the patient free to spend much of his time in the community. Psychiatric social workers, who counsel families on how to deal with disturbed members, help to prevent unnecessary hospitalization and to reintegrate the released patient. Reemployment services, sheltered workshops, and foster homes are other settings in which potential patients and ex-patients are treated outside the hospital.

Undoubtedly the best publicized development in the mental health field, related to the general breakdown of barriers between hospitals and society just described, is the spread of community mental health centers. Established largely through federal funding under the Mental Health Center Act of 1963, the centers are designed, in theory, to involve communities directly in preventing and treating the kinds of behavioral problems that might otherwise lead to segregation of the individual from society. The centers are supposed to provide a wider range of services than the mental hospital or clinic would ordinarily offer, and to reach people whom other mental health facilities fail to reach, particularly the poor. While it is still too early to evaluate the overall effect of the community mental health movement, it is safe to say that it has not brought about the "revolution in mental health care" that some of its early proponents hoped for. Preliminary evaluations conducted for the government (*Behavior Today*, 1972) revealed a number of faults with the centers: many failed to incorporate representatives of the communities, especially poor communities, in positions of genuine power; perhaps as a consequence, many failed to offer the social and educational services that poor clients demand, and adhered instead to the traditional concept of mental illness as a disease to be treated on an individual basis; in general, the centers were not well known to the public or widely used. A more recent review of research on community mental health centers, though still optimistic about the potential of the centers, concurs with the earlier evaluation and concludes that the accomplishments of the first decade of the movement have fallen short of its goals (Bloom, 1973, p. 30). In addition to such problems as reduction in federal funding, the reviewer points out that centers have rarely undertaken innovative programs and rarely documented the effectiveness of their services.

A final set of developments in the mental health field has centered around the legal and civil rights of mental patients. Formerly in most states people could be committed to mental hospitals against their will on the testimony of two doctors. Since the process was construed as medical diagnosis, i.e., testimony by dispassionate experts as to the existence of an objective illness, the potential patient was not thought to require representation by legal counsel, nor was he allowed to present medical witnesses in his own behalf. In some states now the penal nature of involuntary commitment has been recognized, and the commitment hearing takes place in the presence of a judge. The potential patient is represented by a lawyer, and can have doctors, chosen by him, testify to his sanity. Even patients already committed may have the right to appeal and reopen their cases for release.

A related development is the formation of voluntary associations of ex-patients, such as Mental Patients' Resistance and the Mental Patients' Liberation Project. As the militant titles suggest, these organizations aim to produce major changes in commitment procedures and treatment of patients. In addition, they function as self-help groups, offering the released inmate aid in fighting the stigma of ex-patient status, in finding a job, and otherwise getting on his feet.

THE FUTURE: A WORLD WITHOUT WALLS?

We have said much in this chapter that is critical of institutions as settings for reform of criminals or treatment of mental patients. Although we have no blueprint to offer for solving the problems of crime and mental illness, we do feel that some essential elements of a solution have become apparent through America's historical experience with institutional approaches.

The key element in any attack on crime and mental illness must be a recognition of their social character. Mental illness arises when personal relations become intolerable; crime flourishes when the individual is oppressed by poverty and surrounded by a subculture in which criminality is an accepted way of life. This was the fundamental insight of nineteenth-century founders of our systems of prisons and asylums. Without the details supplied by modern social science, they understood that crime and madness grow out of the individual's social surroundings. Of course, crime and mental illness may have important nonsocial elements: biochemical and genetic factors, for example, may be linked to the perceptual distortions and cognitive malfunctioning associated with some forms of mental illness and to the hyperaggressive behavior associated with some forms of crime. But to a large extent it is the reaction of others to the deviant impulse that determines whether it will be elaborated into a set of symptoms or a criminal career, or whether it will be controlled in such a way as to allow the individual to lead a satisfying and socially useful life.

The architects of our corrections and mental health systems erred in locating the *disease* in the individual, despite their wisdom in perceiving its social causes. By segregating the criminal or disturbed person, they thought they could preserve the rest of society, just as the surgeon saves the body by excising the diseased appendix. As for the deviant individual, they thought he could be reformed by being taken out of oppressive conditions and bad company, by being forcibly exposed to the presumed beneficial effects of solitude, hard work, and scripture. On the one hand, they failed to anticipate the ways in which the dynamics of total institutions frustrate the goal of individual reform. On the other hand, they failed to see that removal of the diseased individual did nothing to alleviate the conditions that *caused* his disease. Without real ties to the community, without broad-based public participation in the reform of individual deviants and in the eradication of the social causes of deviance, prisons and asylums could become only dumping grounds for human refuse.

What of the future? Is there any reason to hope that the crucial public participation just mentioned is likely to come about? We have expressed cautious hope, and many reservations, about current attempts to integrate institutional treatment of offenders and patients with the context of the wider society. In part, the motivation for these efforts is sound; the questions, as we saw particularly in the case of community mental health centers, is whether a really effective community base can be built, given the legacy of old ways of thinking about criminals and the mentally ill. Perhaps the men who established our prisons and asylums in the Age of Jackson counted on two factors we cannot count on today: the ideological homogeneity and the intense citizen participation of the small town. Perhaps they simply took for granted the active attempt of people in small communities to reaffirm the common moral order by aiding and educating their troubled or wayward fellows. It is doubtful that either a common moral order or an ethic of mutual responsibility exists in modern urban society.

It seems clear that the trend for the immediate future is toward more community-based activity in mental health and offender rehabilitation. At the same time, it is obvious that institutional treatment will not disappear altogether.

The long-range future of prisons and asylums in the United States is an uncertain one. What is certain, however, is that broader changes in society itself are required if these institutions, or any future versions of them, are to be effective as agents of positive change in individuals. It is to the larger issue of societal change that we now turn.

Chapter 5

Socialization and Change in Society

Man has been fascinated with the construction of utopias, real and imaginary, ever since he began to think seriously about the nature of his society. An important element in utopian thought, especially since the advent of modern psychology, has been the transformation of society through the transformation of the child.

Sociologists and anthropologists agree that two essential functions of any society are (1) the maintenance of internal order and cohesion and (2) the capacity to reproduce itself from generation to generation. *Socialization,* the training of children in the values, roles, and adult behavior patterns of a given culture, is a key process in the achievement of both goals. Order is maintained not primarily through the operation of laws, the police, or kindred institutions of coercion and surveillance, but through shared values and voluntary control of behavior on the part of individuals. Socialization is partially responsible for the fact that individuals in a society, even a deeply divided or pluralistic society such as ours, do share many of the same values and act in accordance with shared standards of right and wrong. At the same time, of course, socialization is partially responsible for the continuity of values across generations. Thus, to speak of change in the socialization process is to speak of change in society itself.

The family and the socialization process are today undergoing widespread reexamination, experimentation, and fundamental change. In our society the traditional middle-class nuclear family—mother, father, and children living under the same roof—and traditional methods and goals of child rearing have come under fire from many sources. For example, feminists attack what they see as an unfair division of labor in the family, which burdens women with chores of housework and child care, thus blocking their other ambitions and talents. They also assail the teaching of sex roles and sex stereotypes to children, which, they hold, build into young females a sense of insecurity, inferiority, and dependence on men. Feminists have been joined by many others in attacking the reverse side of sex role socialization as well—the pressure on the male child to be competitive and aggressive and to measure his personal worth in terms of superiority over others. At the same time a small but highly visible group of people, mostly young, have moved from criticism to action, abandoning the nuclear family structure altogether to live and raise their children in urban and rural communes. Outside our own society bold experiments have been undertaken with radically new modes of child rearing. The Israeli kibbutz, with its collective nurseries, and the Russian educational system, with its close linkage of home, school, and local community in the service of a national ideology, are noteworthy examples. Finally, to add to all this ferment, developmental psychologists have pointed with increasing concern to socialization influences outside the home—the school, the peer group, and, more recently, television.

In short, then, socialization is of central importance for society, and it is undergoing dramatic change, both in this country and abroad. Some of the changes, e.g., the impact of television, are unintended consequences of change in other areas of society. Other changes represent conscious efforts to mold new men who will serve better values and lead better lives than previous generations. Such experiments are perhaps the clearest existing examples of attempts to apply psychology (in this case, developmental psychology) to bring about major social change. In the rest of this chapter, we will take a closer look at some of these important developments. First, however, let us equip ourselves with a few of the theoretical tools and empirical findings of crosscultural child development research.

Child Development in Crosscultural Perspective

Many child psychologists have observed that each society finds ways of raising children so as to produce adults whose personal characteristics are especially adapted to the needs of that society. As we saw in Chapter 2, the classic statement of this position is Erik Erikson's *Childhood and Society* (1950). Erikson's theoretical approach is psychoanalytic; that is, he follows in the intellectual tradition of Sigmund Freud. Unlike many other psychoanalytic theorists, however, Erikson stresses the continuity of development throughout life. He accepts the traditional psychoanalytic insistence on the importance of the early years of life in shaping personality, but he identifies crucial turning points, "crises" as he calls them (the widely known "identity crisis" being one), in later life as well. More germane to our discussion, he is also sensitive to the ways in which differences among cultures affect the nature of the developmental crises as they are experienced by members of those cultures. His theory is highly abstract, but it acquires flesh-and-blood concreteness through his anthropological studies of child rearing in different cultures and his psychobiographies of famous historical figures. He is able, for example, to link the infant feeding and weaning practices of two American Indian cultures to the unique constellation of personal characteristics that each culture traditionally tended to foster: one, the Dakota Sioux, generous, adventurous, warlike hunters; the other, the Yurok of the Pacific coast, possession-oriented fishermen. Erikson's work and a great deal of other work similar in spirit, produced by the "culture and personality" school of anthropologists and psychologists, has firmly established the principle that cultural differences in values, roles, etc., are expressed in socialization practices and that these in turn shape a new generation to carry on those cultural traditions.

This general principle suggests that change in values and roles on the one hand or in socialization practices on the other are interdependent. For example, Erikson details poignantly how the disruption of Indian culture by the white man has shattered the harmonious relationship between Indian child rearing and the world of the Indian adult, a historical development which has taken an ugly toll in apathy and resentment. The principle also entails a corollary: it is clear that every culture not only confers psychological benefits on its members—a sense of identity, community, and personal worth—but also that each extracts some psychological price. In one illustrative study, Erikson describes the extreme subjugation of women in traditional Sioux society, and the cruelty with which the Sioux warrior treated himself and his enemies.

Ideas like these raise a host of important questions and possibilities. Perhaps most crucial for our discussion is the possibility that a society can, by conscious and systematic overhauling of its child care and educational practices, produce spreading ripples of positive change throughout its entire system. Can society *improve* itself by direct intervention in the socialization process, or can it only trade one set of advantages and disadvantages for another?

Freud was something of a pessimist on this score. He spent most of his professional life in the clinic, confronting the irrationalities, the unconscious conflicts, the unacknowledged motives and wishes of troubled people. As a consequence he made the rest of us aware, through his writings, of the role of the instinctual and the irrational in human nature. When he turned his attention to political and social theory, he retained his focus on these aspects of human functioning. Just as he interpreted the particular neuroses of his patients as manifestations of a conflict between innate sexual and aggressive instincts and the demands of European civilization (as manifested in its child-rearing practices), so, more broadly, did he also see the tension of civilization and instinct as inevitable. Although he argued forcefully, e.g., in his essay "Civilized Sexual Morality and Modern Nervous Illness" (Freud, 1953), that a diminishing of sexual repression would bring a reduction in specific neuroses, he held out little hope that psychological suffering would ever disappear. Freud felt that some sexual drives, the *infantile* and *bisexual* ones, were incompatible with a satisfying genital sexuality and with the family, the cornerstone of the social order. More important, he felt that aggressive drives were an obvious threat to civilization and must be renounced in the interest of cultural survival and social harmony. Since the sexual and aggressive drives were seen as largely inborn, Freud felt that civilization must, by its very nature, impose renunciation on the child through the socialization process. Thus a substantial amount of instinctual frustration was a price all men must pay for being human, i.e., *social*, beings. This position was argued most forcefully in his book *Civilization and Its Discontents,* published in 1929-30 (Freud, 1962).

Not all Freudians agree with Freud on these issues. Erikson says little about the subject, but the tenor of some of his remarks is akin to Freud's:

> Undoubtedly each culture ... creates character types marked by its own mixture of defect and excess; and each culture creates rigidities and illusions which protect it against the insight that no ideal, safe, permanent state can emerge from the blueprint it has gropingly evolved. (Erikson, 1950, p. 186)

Still, there is somewhat more room for optimism in Erikson's system than in Freud's. Because Erikson explicitly emphasizes personality development beyond the early years, there is greater potential for significant change in mature people, despite the undenied legacy of early experience. Because Erikson takes account of cultural variation to a greater extent than does Freud, the possibility of choice among alternative patterns of child rearing and modal adult character is more salient in his viewpoint.

A much more radical optimism concerning the possibility of improving society through improved socialization techniques is found in the work of behaviorist B. F. Skinner, whose theories and research on the modification of responses through reinforcement underlie some of the psychotherapeutic techniques discussed in Chapters 2 and 4. Without denying the existence of innate, species-specific behavior patterns, Skinner stresses the modifiability of those patterns through experience. In his novel *Walden Two* (1948), Skinner describes a utopian community founded on behavioral principles. In *Walden Two,* most of the work of child rearing is done not by parents but by psychologically trained staff in collective nurseries. Young infants are carefully protected from all accidental pains and frustrations by being raised nude in sterile, temperature-controlled, padded boxes. Toys, mobiles, and other objects are provided in order to stimulate the child's perceptual and cognitive exploration of the world. Parents and other adults are allowed frequent periods of play with the infant in order to stimulate the beginnings of social development. As the child grows older, he is moved into a collective nursery where systematic "moral and ethical" training is begun. Frustrations are gradually introduced in small, graded doses, and always within the child's capacity to bear and master them. For example, hungry children are required to stand for five minutes in front of steaming bowls of soup before eating. A child who falters is not punished; he is simply exposed to milder frustrations and gradually allowed to build up his tolerance until he is able to master the original task. Skinner believes that, through techniques such as these, children can be taught self-control and restraint over their impulses.

In Chapter 2 we considered some of the ethical objections to behavior modification; many of the same objections have been levied against Skinner's proposals concerning socialization. It is said that his techniques are totalitarian and inhumane, that they deny the freedom and dignity of the individual. Skinner's reply, contained both in *Walden Two* and in his recent bestseller, *Beyond Freedom and Dignity* (1971), is the following: Pain, frustration, and conflicts between impulse and social order are inevitable. When the child encounters these experiences in an accidental and uncontrolled manner, he may be overwhelmed by them and suffer unnecessary fear and suppression of impulse; or, on the other hand, he may become rebellious, selfish, and antisocial. The freedom and dignity of those who successfully navigate a course between these extremes is purchased at the price of many social failures. True freedom and dignity, Skinner argues, can be achieved for everyone through an understanding and application of scientific principles of behavior control.

Thus, the theoretical disputes among contemporary psychologists involve momentous and unsettled practical consequences. There is agreement that the ways in which children are raised is no minor matter, that the very character of society is at stake in the nursery. But there is disagreement concerning the degree to which concomitant changes in social structure and socialization can make man happier or more moral than he is. We will return to this question in our conclusion, after a look at changes in child-rearing practices today.

In the following two sections we consider two examples of attempts to change societies by changing the ways in which children are raised. Both, as it happens, are attempts to build a "new socialist man," in the Soviet Union and on the Israeli kibbutz. We select these examples because they have been studied by Western psychologists and because they present an instructive contrast to child rearing in the U.S. Our choice is not meant to imply that the Russian and Israeli cases are the only ones of their kind (Cuba and Mainland China are other examples), nor that the systematic use of socialization is necessarily confined to socialist systems. (For example, John Dewey argued that education must play a central role in training citizens to participate in American society.) What sets these examples apart from patterns of change in other countries is their planned, systematic, consciously utopian character. Following our discussion of Israel and the USSR we will consider the unplanned but no less significant changes in child rearing now occurring in the United States.

SOCIALIZATION AND PLANNED SOCIAL CHANGE: THE CASE OF THE ISRAELI KIBBUTZ

Probably the most thoroughgoing attempt to remake a society through radical change in the raising of children has been carried out on the Israeli *kibbutz*. The *kibbutzim* are communal villages scattered around the Israeli countryside. They are quite small, ranging in size from less than a hundred to about two thousand inhabitants. Their primary economic activity is farming, though in recent years many kibbutzim have established small industries that contribute significantly to their economies. The earliest kibbutz settlements were founded before the state of Israel itself, by young European Jews who hoped to build socialist communities based on hard physical labor, collective ownership of goods, and radically new forms of social organization in which the family would play a much reduced role. Despite the youth and inexperience of the founders, the harshness of the land, and conflicts with Arab neighbors, the early kibbutzim survived and flourished. The movement grew in size and influence; by the mid-sixties there were some 250 kibbutzim in Israel, with about 80,000 members, or 4 percent of the population of the country.

One of the most striking features of the modern kibbutz, and the one which makes the kibbutz highly relevant for our purposes, is the systematic use of child-rearing practices to mold a new generation of kibbutz dwellers. Collective ideals are conveyed not just by instruction, but by an active way of life—a form of upbringing radically different from that practiced in the American nuclear family. Of course, not all kibbutzim are identical; there are several different "movements" within the broader federation of kibbutzim, and they differ on many points of political philosophy and in many concrete features of social organization, including methods used in the rearing of children. Westerners who have studied child rearing in the kibbutz, chiefly Melford Spiro (1956, 1958) and Bruno Bettelheim (1969) have done intensive case studies of single kibbutzim, and these must be in some respects unique. However, regardless of how typical or atypical the cases may be, they illustrate techniques and effects of collective child rearing in two specific instances. They show us what communal upbringing *can* mean and provide us with rich sources of hypotheses about the relations between child-rearing practices and adult personality.

On the kibbutzim studied by Spiro and Bettelheim, and on many others as well, children live apart from their parents, with others of the same age, from birth on. From the fourth or fifth day after delivery, they are placed in nurseries and cared for by full-time *metapelets,* caretakers or nurses. Each metapelet may care for four to six babies in one room. Their mothers visit periodically to nurse them, and their fathers may also visit in the hours between work and mealtime. From the age of six months or a year, children are taken to visit at their parents' rooms, and this practice of after-work and weekend visits continues into adolescence. When the infant is old enough to walk (about one year) he is transferred to the Toddler's House, where he encounters a new nurse and four to eight other children. Here he is toilet-trained, learns to feed himself, and begins to interact with his peers. Somewhere around the fourth birthday, the child moves to Kindergarten, and usually to a new home. He is cared for by a Kindergarten teacher and, usually, another new nurse. At this time he is made part of a group of sixteen to eighteen children (the *kevutza*) who will remain together until high school, moving as a group from the Kindergarten House to the Children's House where they remain from the age of seven until twelve. In the Children's House they encounter for the first time other children of different ages, although they continue to live with their kevutza, which has its own teacher, classroom, and bedrooms. On completion of the sixth grade, children move to a combined junior high and high school, which, like all their earlier quarters, has its own dormitories and dining facilities. Here the kevutza may be broken up, and the individual may be expected to take part in a self-regulating "youth society" considerably larger, and more independent of direct adult influence, than any of the earlier groups. Upon graduating from high school, both men and women enter the army (military service is universal) for two years of active duty. After this time they may return to the kibbutz and petition for admission as full adult members.

The interest of psychologists and psychiatrists in the kibbutz has centered on the effects of early separation of children from parents, of growing up in the early years without a pair of particular nurturing adults to provide security and guidance. Most psychological theories of child development, especially theories related to Freud's psychoanalytic approach, have stressed the importance of parents as models with whom children can identify, whose values and behavior the child can emulate. Generally, primary attachment, the emotional bond between mother and child, is seen as a necessary base for all future social relations, and the continued presence of a parent of the same sex as the child is considered to provide an important role model.

Given the presumed importance of the early years in the development of these basic elements of personality, and given the role attributed to caretakers in the process, psychologists naturally wondered about the effects of communal child rearing in the kibbutz. Would the much-reduced contact with the child's mother and the constant switching of metapelets rob the child of a stable adult figure with whom he could form the emotional bond of attachment? Would the limited contact with fathers rob little boys of appropriate objects for identification? Would the division of the metapelet's attention among the group leave individual children starved for security and affection? If any or all of these conjectures proved true, what dire effects could be observed in the children's behavior and in their adult personalities?

The observations of Spiro and especially Bettelheim make it clear that extravagant fears about kibbutz child rearing are groundless. Psychopathology is not rampant on the kibbutz among children or among kibbutz-born adults. Both Bettelheim and Spiro found the *sabras,* young kibbutz-born adults, to be hardworking, productive people, mostly of average-to-high intellectual ability, with strong consciences and fierce loyalties to their peers, to the kibbutz, and to Israel. Although the level of aggression among children and adolescents seemed high to Spiro, crime and antisocial behavior among adults were virtually absent.

To conclude that the kibbutz is not a breeding ground for psychopathology is not, however, to claim that communal child rearing is without its psychological price. Two important negative aspects of adult sabra personality are noted by both Spiro and Bettelheim. The first is an excessive (to American eyes) dependency of the sabra on his peer group. According to both observers, the kibbutz-born tend to feel insecure and undirected without the comforting presence of the tight cohort of age-mates with whom they were raised. A second negative feature is what both observers agree seems to be a "flattening of affect." The sabras seem, again by American standards, to lack the ability to express emotions and to form intimate personal relations. Relations in the peer group are characterized by general camaraderie, but not by close personal bonds and mutual revelation of intimate thoughts and feelings.

The books by Bettelheim and Spiro are fascinating and immensely detailed. We have not begun to scratch the surface of their observations with our brief summary. The interested reader will have to go to the original sources for a fuller picture of kibbutz life. However, it does seem true to the spirit of both books to conclude that the kibbutz appears as a viable alternative to our own way of living. Unlike the many short-lived utopian communities founded by idealists throughout history, the kibbutzim have created in their child-rearing practices a way of perpetuating themselves and their ideals. Those child-rearing practices, like our own, exact a toll from the children of the kibbutz, but they offer unique compensations as well.

SOCIALIZATION AND PLANNED SOCIAL CHANGE: THE CASE OF THE SOVIET UNION

The Israeli kibbutz is a small, cohesive, rural community. There is ample reason to question whether socialization techniques adapted to that type of society can be applied on a larger scale, to an ethnically diverse industrialized nation such as ours. In light of this question, it is instructive to consider the child-rearing practices and educational system of the Soviet Union, a nation ideologically close to the kibbutz in many ways but similar in size, diversity, and world prominence to ours. The USSR is no utopia; nevertheless her attempts to use socialization systematically in the service of the state and of the national ideology makes her an appropriate subject for study in this context.

Urie Bronfenbrenner's *Two Worlds of Childhood: U.S. and U.S.S.R.* (1970) is a provocative comparison of the observed and likely psychological effects of our style of socialization and theirs. During the sixties, Bronfenbrenner made seven visits to the Soviet Union to study Russian methods of upbringing. He interviewed Soviet children, educators, and psychologists, scrutinized teachers' and parents' manuals and other documents, observed children in nurseries and schools, and even conducted a few formal experiments with Russian children (the results of which were then compared with those of similar experiments performed with children in other European countries and the United States).

Bronfenbrenner begins his description of Soviet child rearing with a discussion of the family. He observes that Russian babies and children are exposed to a great deal of physical contact—hugging, kissing, cuddling—and, by American standards, close supervision and considerable worry about the child's welfare. Both affection and concern are shown not only by parents but also by relatives and even by total strangers. At the same time, the child is subject to strict demands for obedience and self-discipline. Although widely read Soviet manuals on child rearing advocate such strict standards of conduct, physical punishment is ruled out; reprimands, shaming, expressions of indignation and hurt by the parents are recommended. These are precisely the kinds of "love-oriented" discipline techniques that American psychologists have found most effective in instilling a high degree of obedience and conformity. (See, for example, Sears, Maccoby, and Levin, 1957.)

The twin emphases on warmth and discipline, of course, exist in many American families and do not in themselves distinguish the Soviet approach to child rearing from our own. What *is* different about Russian child rearing is the much more explicit role of state-run educational institutions in the socialization process. The family and the school are seen as engaged in a cooperative venture, building the model Soviet citizen or "socialist man." Of course similar sentiments about the general role of education in society are sometimes expressed by American parents and educators, but, as Bronfenbrenner attempts to demonstrate, the ideal in Russia is connected to concrete and monolithic institutional reality.

Soviet schools, as Bronfenbrenner describes them, are the subject of much national attention. The goals and methods of the schools are spelled out in detail in official manuals prepared by the national Academy of Pedagogical Sciences. These not only deal with curricular matters and classroom discipline, narrowly conceived, but also contain elaborate prescriptions for moral education, including lists of specific activities appropriate for children of different ages for developing "Communist morality, a responsible attitude toward learning, cultural conduct, esthetic culture, and physical culture." The specific activities are not confined to the classroom; they cover behavior at home and in public places as well. For Grade I (age seven), some of the prescriptions offered are the following:

In school. All pupils are to arrive at school and in the classroom on time, wipe their feet upon entering, greet the teacher and all technical staff by name . . . keep one's things in order, obey all instructions of the teacher, learn rules of class conduct . . . learn and fulfill special classroom duties such as those of monitor, sanitarian, class librarian. . . .

At home. Upon rising, greet one's parents, thank them after the meal or for any help received; before leaving, check to make sure you have everything necessary; upon return from school, put everything in its place; take care of your own things (e.g., sew on buttons, iron, shine shoes . . .), in accordance with ability, help with housecleaning, dusting. . . .

In public places. Behave calmly; obey all requests of elders, do not disturb others by loud noise or running; . . . don't litter. . . . (Academy of Pedagogical Sciences, USSR, *The Program of the Upbringing Work of the School.* Quoted in Bronfenbrenner, 1970, pp. 26-27.)

The recommended activities for older children are similar, though naturally the tasks designated are somewhat different. Twelve-year-olds, for example, are exhorted to "assist the teacher in setting up visual aids and uncomplicated instructional materials; keep a daily notebook of all work and submit it regularly for examination and signature by parents . . . participate in getting fuel for heating the school (chopping wood) . . ." etc.

Two facts about these activity lists are striking to the Western eye, at least to the Western eyes of the present authors. The first is that the regimentation recommended for Soviet school children is more severe than most American schools would dare impose. Children are expected to rise when reciting, to greet all adults formally, and so forth. The second is that the concrete activities that are held to build "Communist morality" are very much the same as those that are supposed to build "Protestant" or "American" virtues—hard work, respect for elders, cheerfulness, honesty, etc. There are, however, several important differences in the behavior expected of children, in the values taught, and in the social organizations to which children are exposed.

At the level of values, the difference lies in the Soviet emphasis on *collectivism.* To the degree that children are capable of understanding such matters, they are taught that specific rules of behavior—good manners, dedication to school work and to school and household chores, care of public property, etc.—all flow naturally from a socialist ethic of collective ownership, effort, and responsibility.

At the level of behavior and day-to-day interaction, perhaps the most striking difference between the Soviet school and our own lies in the use of peers as an instrument of school (and, by extension, national) policy. When Russian children are urged to strive for excellence, the goal is not individual but group glory. The teacher is urged to achieve order by challenging the children "Let's see *which row* can sit straightest" (italics added). Academic honors are similarly computed for rows within the classroom, classrooms within the school, schools within the geographic region. When a row or larger group does poorly, blame falls not only on the slow student whose performance has detracted from the group's showing but also on the bright student who failed to help his duller comrade. Discipline problems such as chronic lateness or disruptiveness are handled by enlisting classmates to pressure the unruly individual into compliance. The systematic direction of the Soviet peer group by adults stands in sharp contrast to American adolescent peer groups, which tend to operate independently of adult influence and to adopt values in partial opposition to those of the school. In addition, whole classes of older children "adopt" classes of younger children, and take responsibility for tutoring and disciplining them. The older classes may in turn be adopted by adult groups, such as workers in a factory shop or on a collective farm. This practice of group adoption, *shevstvo,* is designed to involve the community at large in the process of education.

At the level of formal organizations, virtually all Russian children are members of one of two state-sponsored youth groups, the Octobrists (ages seven to nine) or the Pioneers (ages ten to fifteen). The aims of these organizations are identical with those of the school, and each classroom is a "cell" of the organization appropriate for the age level of its students. The uniforms, posters, and slogans of these organizations bear a striking resemblance to those of the Boy and Girl Scouts in this country. Again, however, a key difference is that the organizations are run by the state and ideologically linked to the Party, and membership is essentially compulsory. The Pioneers serve as a feeder group for the Komsomol, or Young Communist League, for youths fifteen to twenty-eight. (The Komsomol is selective and enrolls only about half the youths eligible by age.) Bronfenbrenner's account implies that many of the organized leisure-time activities of Soviet children and adolescents take place in the context of one of these formal groups. Thus these organizations are another strand in the web of family, school, and state that enmeshes the growing child from birth and carefully guides his development.

Bronfenbrenner's description of the Russian educational system is fascinating, but one important element is missing from our recounting of it, namely, the actual behavior of the children involved. Regardless of what the manuals for parents and teachers say, regardless even of what parents and teachers may put into practice, the success or failure of any system of child rearing must be measured in terms of the attitudes and actions of the children. Much of the information Bronfenbrenner provides on this key question is informal and anecdotal. (This was of course a necessity imposed by the conditions under which he made his many observations.) On the whole, his observations in classrooms seem to have confirmed the efficacy of the system. Order, obedience, cheerfulness, and good relations between adults and children seem to be the rule in Soviet schools. Aggressiveness, violation of rules, and other instances of antisocial behavior were rare. Particularly striking are his examples of cases in which children were disciplined by other children (Bronfenbrenner, 1970, pp. 63-68); the personal remorse and shame felt by the "wrongdoers" stand in sharp contrast to the resentful and unrepentant response of many American children to discipline by adults. Are such examples typical or misleading? We can only take the word of a concerned and honest observer that, so far as he could determine, they were typical.

However, Bronfenbrenner's account of the behavior of Soviet children does not rest entirely on anecdotes. He performed a series of experiments with many hundreds of twelve-year-old children from the USSR and other countries, examining their responses to questions about how they would react to opportunities for misbehavior, or to actual misbehavior on the part of others, and about the personal qualities they valued most. (Some of the studies are summarized in Bronfenbrenner, 1970, pp. 77–81; two of them are reported in detail by Bronfenbrenner, 1967; and by Rodgers et al., 1968.)

In one study, concerned with peer group pressure (Bronfenbrenner, 1967), children were asked what they would do if friends urged them to participate in some forbidden act such as cheating on a test, stealing fruit, or wearing clothes their parents disapproved of. Soviet children were much less likely to say that they would go along with their friends than American children. An interesting comparison was added to the study by telling some of the children that the results of the experiment would be anonymous, seen only by the researchers, while others were told that the results would be shown to parents and teachers, and a third group that they would be seen by other children. Not surprisingly, both Soviet and American children expressed less willingness to participate in the forbidden activities when they thought parents and teachers would see their answers than when they thought only the researchers would see them. However, the prospect of having other children see the results produced different outcomes in the two countries: American children expressed *more* willingness to misbehave, while Russian children expressed *less,* when other children would see their responses than when the responses were anonymous. (All the shifts in responses induced by the anticipated "audiences" were small relative to the very large differences between Soviet and American groups across all experimental conditions.)

The results of this and other studies, together with Bronfenbrenner's observations in Soviet classrooms, strongly suggest that Soviet methods of "character education" significantly affect Soviet children. At least as reported by the children themselves, their behavior and values appear to differ measurably from those of Western European and American groups. Does this mean that Soviet methods of education are "better" than those of the West? This of course is not a question the psychologist-*as-psychologist* can answer, although the psychologist-as-citizen can and should have an opinion. To answer such a question requires us to place a value judgment on the facts, and this is particularly difficult in the case at hand. Soviet methods seem to produce cooperative, nonaggressive, idealistic individuals who are also conforming and submissive to authority. Americans tend to place a positive value on the first set of characteristics and a negative judgment on the second. If we have gone too far in the direction of assertive, competitive individuality, so, it seems, the Soviets have gone too far in the opposite direction. We will return to this issue in our conclusion, after a look at changing patterns of socialization in our own society.

THE CHANGING AMERICAN CHILD

Our investigation of changing patterns of child training ends at home, with a selective review of significant alterations in the American style of socialization. In contrast to the cases of Israel and the USSR, changes in the United States have largely been unplanned; no one labored or conspired to bring them about. Indeed, many observers see little good in their effects and hope that they can be reversed or offset.

Bronfenbrenner's (1970) treatment of American child rearing provides the framework for our discussion. He identifies several major trends: the decline of the family as the central agent of socialization, accompanied by an increase in the influence of peers, television, and the school.

Bronfenbrenner sees the reduced role of the family as an abdication of responsibility on the part of American adults. Yet he views this abdication not as a conscious or deliberate act, but as a consequence of social changes beyond the control of most families. One such change is the breakup of the extended family; grandparents, aunts and uncles no longer live under the same roof with, or in close proximity to, the nuclear family. A related change is the shift from small-town to urban and suburban living. No longer is the town or neighborhood a cohesive, self-sufficient social unit in which people all know one another and shop at the same grocery store, go to the same movie house, etc. Instead, families are isolated units, and they tend to drive relatively long distances to shops, recreation, friends, and so forth. Thus children are not surrounded by friendly, concerned adults as they once were (and as they still are in small towns, according to research cited by Bronfenbrenner).

This situation, however, has not brought children into closer company with their parents. Fathers are likely to commute to work some distance from home, and to work many weekends as well. Mothers are increasingly likely to have jobs or to be involved in community work. Also, more and more recreational activities are age-segregated, as when boys play little league baseball rather than going fishing with their fathers. Thus the typical child's contact with adults in general, and parents in particular, is diminished.

Believing that adult models and guides are crucial for the healthy development of the child, Bronfenbrenner fears that the lack of contact between children and adults can be disastrous. He warns that ". . . we can anticipate increased alienation, indifference, antagonism and violence on the part of the younger generation in all segments of our society—middle-class children as well as the disadvantaged" (Bronfenbrenner, 1970, p. 117). In support of this view he cites research concerned with the effects on children of the absence of one or both parents, usually the father. Different studies have examined different aspects of child behavior and attitudes, so no simple summary of all these findings can be given; however, it is safe to say that the effects of parental absence have been found to be negative, in varying degrees. In Bronfenbrenner's words, "In general, father absence contributes to low motivation for achievement, inability to defer immediate rewards for later benefits, low self esteem . . . and juvenile delinquency" (Bronfenbrenner, 1970, p. 104). Bronfenbrenner also makes the point that the parent need not be absent permanently or under special circumstances, as were the fathers in most of the studies cited above. In research of his own, he found that children from American two-parent middle-class families who reported that their parents were away from home for long periods rated significantly lower than others in "responsibility" and "leadership."

As contact with adults diminishes, children are left to a greater degree than ever before in the company of peers of the same age as well as with a powerful new influence—the television set. At the same time there is an increase in the importance of school, the only adult institution capable of filling the vacuum left by the family. In the following sections we examine more closely these increasingly important sources of socialization.

Peers as Socializers

Bronfenbrenner (1970, p. 101) reports a study in which he and two associates asked over seven hundred sixth-graders whom they spent their time with on weekends. The children reported spending two to three hours per day with their parents, and about twice this much time with friends. Moreover, when asked whom they *preferred* to spend time with, many more chose friends than parents. The study demonstrates that the importance of peers is well established by the age of eleven and, at least in terms of sheer time spent, outweighs that of parents.

Similar implications are evident in several other studies as well. Sociologists Charles Bowerman and John Kinch (1959) investigated 686 students in the fourth through tenth grades of a school district near Seattle, Washington. The investigators asked their subjects whether they preferred to spend time with parents or peers, whether they thought parents or peers understood them better, whether they wanted to be more like their parents or their friends, and whether they agreed more closely with parents or friends about what was right and wrong in a variety of situations. On the basis of these responses, each subject was given an overall rating of peer-priented, family-oriented, or neutral. The researchers found that 87 percent of the fourth-graders were family-oriented and that the percentage dropped with age to 32 percent in the tenth grade. In a study performed in 1968 by two associates of Bronfenbrenner (1970, p. 105) a substantially greater amount of peer dependence was found at every age and grade level than in the Bowerman and Kinch study. Bronfenbrenner concludes that the importance of peers as socializers increases with age and also is increasing over time, as parents devote less time and effort to their children.

Are these trends cause for alarm? Bronfenbrenner thinks they are. As we have seen, he believes that adult socializers are crucial for the development of character, and he has serious reservations about the kinds of values the peer group tends to communicate. An important line of evidence that leads Bronfenbrenner to question the value of the peer group as a socializing agent comes from *The Adolescent Society,* a book published in 1961 by James Coleman. Coleman's study covered a wide range of attitudes and behaviors among students in eight large high schools during the late fifties and very early sixties. In the typical school Coleman found that a "leading crowd" could be identified, a group who set the tone and style for others in the school. Boys in the leading crowd were usually athletes; girls were "popular dates." The value placed on intellectual ability or academic achievement varied from school to school. In some schools it was actually a detriment to one's status; nowhere was it more than a minor "plus." The peer group, Coleman's study implies, stresses the shallowest of values and flies in the face of adult values and socialization efforts.

There are, then, substantial reasons behind Bronfenbrenner's concern about the apparent increase in the influence of the peer group among American children and adolescents. Before leaving this topic, however, we should point out several facts that tend to qualify Bronfenbrenner's position. First, not all developmental psychologists find a gap between the values of peers and parents. In fact, in a recent comprehensive review of the research literature concerning the effects of peers on the growing child, Willard Hartup (1970) concludes that most studies indicate that "peer values are basically consonant with adult values" (p. 429). The child may be more influenced by peers than parents as he grows older, but the peer group is not likely to put him into the bitter conflict with his parents that is often assumed to exist in adolescence. Even young radical political activists, usually assumed to be rebels against their parents or society, in fact typically come from homes in which liberal-to-radical political beliefs are espoused. This point is forcefully made, for example, through Kenneth Keniston's case studies in *Young Radicals* (1968) and David Rosenhan's work on civil rights activists (1970). Second, Bronfenbrenner relies mainly on data collected a decade or more ago. In his 1970 book he says nothing about the youth culture of the late sixties, nothing about hippies or radical political activism, nothing about love-ins or peace marches. Surely these activities must be heavily influenced by peers, and perhaps in some of their social-structural features they bear a resemblance to the activities of adolescent cliques and crowds in the past. But surely there are important differences in purpose and style as well. In short, more needs to be discovered about the widening role of peers in socialization.

The Tube as Tutor

Of all the forces that compete with parents in socializing children, one that has aroused special public concern is television. The reasons for this concern are easy to see: according to at least two studies (Bailyn, 1959; Lyle & Hoffman, 1971) the average American child between the ages of six and sixteen watches about *twenty-two* hours of television per week, far more time than he spends in any other activity except sleep, play, and school. By the age of sixteen, the average person has watched a total of 12,000 to 15,000 hours of television. The sheer amount of time involved would naturally lead parents, psychologists, and educators to wonder if that time was being spent constructively, even if there were no other causes for concern.

Of course, there are other causes, and one in particular has generated abundant polemics, namely the effect of televised violence on children. Four of the five research volumes of the 1971 report of the Surgeon General's Scientific Advisory Committee on Television and Social Behavior (1972) are devoted exclusively to this topic, and many other studies on the subject have appeared earlier in psychological journals. Unfortunately, this mass of research has not led to unequivocal conclusions, as a look at the summary of the Surgeon General's report will suggest. There is no question that the amount of violence in TV programming is high—the Surgeon General's report found about eight such instances *per hour* among "story" shows telecast over the three major networks. The question is whether exposure to fictionalized instances of violence increases the likelihood that people, particularly children, will engage in violent or aggressive behavior.

Critics of the media point out that the imitative propensities of children are well known and that they can therefore be expected to copy what they see. More subtly, when heroes right wrongs by violent means, children are taught that violence is an acceptable way of settling disputes and that aggressiveness is a desirable feature of the male role. Skeptics counter that the effects of TV, if any, are likely to be minor, that the sources of violence lie elsewhere in society, and that only children already predisposed toward aggressiveness or instability are likely to be so affected by television. Some psychologists have even argued that TV has a cathartic effect, that is, it provides a fantasy outlet for violent impulses and thus actually reduces the level of overt violence in everyday social behavior. All three positions find some measure of support in existing psychological research, although it is clear that the weight of the evidence is on the side of those who fear the effects of TV violence.

There are basically two strategies for research on the subject. The first is a strategy based on laboratory experimentation. In such studies, groups of children are systematically exposed to identical instances of aggressive behavior on film or videotape, while other, "control" groups are exposed to nonaggressive films or tapes, or simply left alone. The behavior of the experimental and control groups is then compared in some situation in which the opportunity for violent or aggressive behavior exists. Typical of this type of research is the widely read work of Albert Bandura and his colleagues (e.g., Bandura et al., 1963). Bandura et al. showed children films of an adult model or of a cartoon character striking and insulting a "Bobo doll," a plastic toy that bounces back to an upright position when hit, and also throwing and breaking other toys and dolls, with accompanying aggressive verbalizations. Afterward the children were left alone (under secret observation) to play in a roomful of toys similar to those in the film. Children who had seen aggressive models on film, whether live adults or cartoon characters, showed significantly more aggressive and destructive behavior in the free-play situation than children who had not seen such film. Often their behavior was an obvious copy of the behavior of the models, and often it seemed to be accompanied by aggressive emotion. Bandura's findings are typical; the Surgeon General's Report refers to some thirty studies, all of which support the claim that children can be stimulated to apparently aggressive behavior by viewing violent TV shorts or films in the lab.

What the laboratory studies leave unclear, however, is the degree to which their findings apply to real-life situations. Children rarely have the opportunity to ape violent acts in situations exactly like those shown on television immediately after turning off the set. Do the effects of aggressive stimulation carry over longer periods of time? Do they apply to forms of aggression unlike the ones seen on TV? Is aggressive *play* of the type studied by Bandura really aggression? Bronfenbrenner (1970, pp. 109-115) examines these questions and concludes that the laboratory results *are* generally applicable. He cites, among others, studies showing that effects of viewing an aggressive film can still be detected six months later, that children rated as aggressive by their peers also preferred aggressive content in TV programs, and that adolescents and adults exposed to violent films were more willing than others to administer painful electric shocks to a protesting victim. (The "victim," of course, was an actor, and the "shocks," fake; the situation was contrived by psychologists to simulate a real-life opportunity for aggression.)

The second strategy of research on TV violence is the field survey. In field surveys, the researcher does not create a controlled situation to study the effects in which he is interested; rather, he attempts to find ways of comparing groups of people in ordinary life situations that will give him the same information. An example is the study mentioned just above, in which the TV program preferences of children (as noted by their parents) and their aggressive behavior (as rated by their peers) were compared. (That study was published by Leonard Eron in 1963.) Like most field studies on the effects of TV violence, Eron's establishes an association or correlation between two different aspects of behavior —viewing violent programs and engaging in a variety of actions that can be labeled aggressive. Surveying a range of similar studies, the Surgeon General's Report summarizes them as pointing to generally positive, but weak, relations between TV violence and children's aggressive behavior.

Beyond the weakness of the results, several other qualifications must be noted. First, correlational studies cannot establish the causal relations among variables. Eron's result, for example, might mean that televised aggression stimulates aggression toward peers, but it might also mean that children who are aggressive for other reasons select TV programs with high aggressive content. This is an example of one way in which field studies sometimes pay a price in logical clarity for their true-to-life quality. Second, several field studies support the latter interpretation of the association between aggressiveness and viewing of violent TV programs in that they show relations between certain personality predispositions and the tendency to view aggressive programs. (Both the Surgeon General's Report and Seymour Feshbach's 1970 review of studies on child aggression cite such studies.) Finally, at least one large-scale field study found no important negative effects of television: Himmelweit et al. (1958) studied 1854 British children, aged ten to fourteen. Some had television in their homes, and others did not. Children from the two groups were selected in matched pairs, each having similar background characteristics and, mostly, coming from the same classrooms. (It would be difficult if not impossible to perform such a study in America today since 96 percent of American homes have TV sets, and those that do not bear little resemblance to the rest of the population who do!) The matched groups of children were then compared on several measures of aggression, delinquency, and maladjustment. No differences were found between TV viewers and nonviewers on these measures. Of course this finding might reflect differences in the content of British as opposed to American television, and no one could argue that the nonviewers in the study really had *no* opportunity to watch TV. Nevertheless, all field studies to a greater or lesser degree involve problems of interpretation; thus, the negative evidence on TV violence (or any other subject) must be weighed along with the positive.

There is one final study on TV violence that deserves discussion here. It is a study interesting for its methodology, since it combines elements of both field and laboratory research, and interesting for its results, since its findings run counter to most of the experimental work in the field. The study was conducted by Seymour Feshbach and Robert D. Singer (1971). The subjects were 665 boys, ranging in age from ten to seventeen years, in seven different institutional settings including private schools, a military school, and boys' homes. Within each institution, two groups of boys were randomly selected; one group was assigned for six weeks to a TV diet that included programs with high aggressive content, while the other group was assigned to programs with (almost) exclusively nonaggressive content. Questionnaire measures of aggression-related personality traits were administered before and after the six-week period. In addition, peers noted each boy's aggressiveness before and after the experiment, and each boy's supervisor made daily ratings of his behavior throughout the test period. Finally, a measure of aggressive *fantasy* was administered at the beginning and end of the period. The boys were shown pictures of a variety of commonplace interpersonal situations and asked to tell stories about the pictures. (This is the so-called Thematic Apperception Test, or TAT.) The stories were then rated for aggressive content.

Feshbach and Singer's results were surprising to most workers in the field. The frequency of verbal and physical aggression, directed toward both peers and authority figures, was *higher* for the control group exposed to nonaggressive TV than for the boys who saw high-aggression programs. (This effect clearly occurred in the boys' homes, but was slight in the private schools. The difference was greatest among boys who were relatively aggressive on the initial personality measures.) Only on the TAT fantasy measure did the violent-TV group show more aggression than the controls. The findings seem to lend support to the catharsis theory of TV aggression: under some circumstances violent TV may provide a fantasy outlet that reduces the level of actual aggressive behavior.

However, the Feshbach & Singer study must be interpreted with caution. It is large in scale and ambitious in scope, but it does seem to be contradicted by many other studies. Moreover, it has been criticized on methodological grounds. (See Liebert et al., 1971 and the replies by Feshbach & Singer, 1971.) Perhaps the most serious criticism of the study has to do with its short-term nature and with the ages of the boys involved. The subjects surely had been exposed to a great deal of violent television throughout their lives, and it might have been unreasonable to expect that a few weeks' confinement to a nonviolent TV diet could offset the effects of those years of exposure. It may even be the case that the increased aggression among those confined to nonviolent shows was caused by frustration at being prevented from watching their favorite programs (although Feshbach & Singer reported that both the violent TV and nonviolent TV groups rated their shows equally high in enjoyability).

On balance, it is clear that there is ample basis in current psychological research for the fears expressed by Urie Bronfenbrenner and many others regarding the growing role of TV in the socialization of American children. Whatever our eventual understanding of the impact of television, Bronfenbrenner is surely right in arguing that the expansion of the media in the lives of children is a development that cannot be responsibly ignored.

Before switching from TV to other subjects, we should also point out that there have been efforts to use the medium as a constructive agent of socialization. The most famous example is the program "Sesame Street," produced by the Children's Television Workshop and broadcast nationally over public television stations. "Sesame Street" is a kaleidoscope of characters and situations designed to entertain as well as instruct preschool children. The program aims at conveying cognitive skills such as the ability to count and recite the alphabet, distinguish perceptual forms, understand logical relationships, classify and order, and master basic ideas about self and society. The program represents an unusual cooperative venture of psychologists with creative and technically skilled people in the TV business. (See Lesser, 1972, for a discussion of the program, its aims, and the process of its creation.) Much research is currently underway on the effectiveness of "Sesame Street"; preliminary data give reason for optimism regarding this attempt to make positive use of a potentially powerful medium.

School as a Socializer

Most children and adolescents spend about six hours a day, five days a week, nine months a year in school from the age of five or six until the age of seventeen or eighteen. Many young people, of course, spend additional years in college and graduate school. We suggested earlier that school, as the only adult-run institution outside the home that occupies so much of the child's day, may fill some of the "socialization gap" left by the parents. If this is true, it is important to examine the kinds of values and roles the modern American school inculcates.

Let us look first at the stated goals of the school system. Everyone agrees that the aim of school is to "educate," but the term means different things to different people. Surely part of almost everyone's definition is the teaching of specific intellectual skills and bodies of knowledge: mathematics, science, history, languages, the familiar list. But almost no educator would stop his definition there. Almost invariably, additional, less tangible goals are cited and often these, not the communication of specific knowledge or skills, are seen as the true, central, or overarching aims of education. Equipping people to function in a modern economy, preparing an informed citizenry, fostering intellectual curiosity, independence, and growth, encouraging self-knowledge and an understanding of others, providing an equal opportunity for all to advance themselves regardless of race or social class background—these are among the broad and idealistic stated aims of American education. In part the goals of school are seen as *instrumental*, preparing the student for some later activity such as work or citizenship; in part they are seen as *intrinsic*, creating in the student desirable qualities of mind.

If the reality of the school system came close to meeting these comprehensive and lofty aims, perhaps Bronfenbrenner's observation of the declining role of parents in socialization would be no cause for concern. We could rest assured that the school was filling the gap admirably. Unfortunately, few observers of the educational system would agree that its goals are being met.

Most attempts by psychologists and other social scientists to evaluate the performance of the schools have concentrated on *cognitive skills,* the kinds of knowledge and abilities so many educators see as means, or secondary goals, rather than ultimate ends. Much of the concern with respect to cognitive skills has focused on the inequalities in skills exhibited by children from poor and middle-class backgrounds. Perhaps the definitive body of data on the subject is the truly massive study by Coleman et al. (1966) of over 600,000 school children at all levels of age, income, and ability, from schools of many different kinds distributed over all regions of the country. On a battery of skill and achievement tests (not tests of intelligence, attitudes, or character) Coleman et al. found that black, Indian-American, Mexican-American, and Puerto Rican children—all children of economically deprived groups— score substantially lower than whites. In both the first and twelfth grades, about 85 percent of these children fall below the white average. This constant *relative* gap represents a widening dispersion of skills: in the third grade, for example, the average black child is one year behind the average white; by the twelfth grade, the gap has widened to three years.

Since it is not our purpose here to investigate the cognitive aspects of schooling, but rather the effects of school as a socializing agent, we will pursue only one of the many ramifications of the Coleman Report. (The interested reader might look at the Report itself, and then at the critiques and extensions of the Report contained in the 1972 collection edited by Mosteller and Moynihan.) Coleman found that children's achievement was affected hardly at all by differences in the quality of their schools as measured by conventional indices such as facilities, class size, or per-pupil expenditures. (Teacher qualifications were one school-related factor that did have some effect, although a surprisingly weak one.) The most powerful influence on children's achievement was the social class composition of the school: predominately middle-class schools produced higher achievement than schools that served impoverished families—and this finding held true even for poor children who happened to attend middle-class schools. These findings suggest, without conclusively proving, that variations in the social climate of the schools —whether in the treatment of children by teachers, or in the interactions among children—are the key determinants of scholastic achievement.

There is some evidence, then, that the school's role as a socializer is as important as its role as a conveyor of skills. It is therefore important to consider *what* values the school inculcates and the processes by which those values are conveyed.

Sociologist Robert Dreeben has studied the school as a social system, with an eye toward the norms, or general standards of conduct that it teaches (Dreeben, 1968). He has identified four such norms as the primary contribution of the school of socialization—*independence, achievement, universalism,* and *specificity.* By independence he means that the student learns to work alone and to expect to be evaluated as an individual. For students to work together, at least on academic tasks like papers and tests, is cheating. By achievement, Dreeben means that students are taught to seek mastery over the environment and strive to meet standards of excellence. (He cites competitive sports and other extracurricular activities, together with classroom work, as areas in which students are encouraged to meet standards of achievement.) The two related concepts of universalism and specificity are derived from the sociological theories of Talcott Parsons. Universalism means that the student is taught to evaluate himself and others according to general, impersonal standards that apply equally to everyone; he is taught not to expect special treatment because of who he is or what special characteristics he may have. Thus, for example, a history test is given to everyone in the class and ostensibly scored by the same standards in every case. Specificity refers to the range of qualities of another person that are relevant for a given social relationship; a *specific* relationship is one in which only one or a few aspects of another person's behavior matter to us. For example, the teacher-student relation is said to be relatively specific in that the student (supposedly) cares principally about the teacher's command of the subject matter and ability to communicate it, while the teacher cares about the student's ability and willingness to learn. Most aspects of the personal lives of both teacher and student are irrelevant to their "professional" relationship. Dreeben points out that the school's emphasis on universalism and specificity is important because many relations in modern society have these characteristics, whereas the child's preschool social relationships in the family stress the opposite norms: the child is treated as a particular person (and not as a member of a category) and almost all of his personal characteristics play a part in his relations with his parents.

Several things need to be said by way of qualification and amplification of Dreeben's catalogue of norms taught in school. First, these norms are not necessarily taught explicitly or systematically. They are a partially hidden curriculum conveyed by the very structure of the school itself and the relations between students and teachers. The teacher is not likely to deliver a lecture on specificity; he teaches it when he ignores Joey's black skin or Mary's pretty smile or Johny's rich father when he marks the math test. Second, these standards are not always met by teachers in practice, even when they are held up as ideals. Clearly, teachers sometimes "play favorites" (violating the norm of universalism); clearly they allow irrelevant personal characteristics, such as race, to creep into their evaluations of academic performance (violating the norm of specificity). Third, these norms are not universally accepted even in theory. For example, when a teacher speaks of tailoring the curriculum or evaluation standards to the needs and characteristics of the individual student, he is upholding a norm of *particularism* rather than universalism.

The latter example should make it clear that none of the norms identified by Dreeben is unqualifiedly "good," nor are their opposites "bad." To the extent that school actually fosters these norms, it is selecting one set of values at the expense of another set with equal, or perhaps greater, claim to legitimacy. We are all so sufficiently used to these norms, especially independence and achievement, in academic settings that we hardly question them. However, it is important to see that other concepts of the student role are possible too. Consider independence, for example. In most of the tasks adults face in everyday life, there is nothing wrong in seeking help from friends, experts, books, etc. In fact, it is considered foolish not to seek such help, and a person who knows how to get it is seen as resourceful, not dishonest. Is it clear, then, that cooperative performance on academic tasks is inappropriate for school children? We have seen in our discussion of the Russian educational system that another approach is possible.

Dreeben's book maintains a tone of academic neutrality. He identifies the norms of the school system without passing judgment on them. (He does, however, point to inconsistencies between the norms of school and the practices of other sectors of society. The above discussion of independence is derived from his.) However, other observers of socialization in the schools have been forthright in attacking those norms.

One such critic is Charles Silberman, whose *Crisis in the Classroom* (1970) was a best-selling examination of some of the faults of American education and some of their possible remedies. Among other indictments, Silberman charges the schools with "educating for docility." He says:

The most important characteristic schools share in common is a preoccupation with order and control. In part, this preoccupation grows out of the fact that school is a collective experience requiring, in the minds of those who run it, subordination of individual to collective or institutional desires and objectives. (Silberman, 1970, p. 122)

Silberman drives his point home with a plethora of examples, all of which will be familiar to recent high school graduates: the lockstep of the school day, with its schedule regulated by bells, the hall passes and john passes, the neat rows of desks where groups of thirty or more young individuals are expected to learn the same things at precisely the same times, etc. Silberman argues plausibly that institutional arrangements like these teach conformity, obedience, and submissiveness regardless of any stated goals of fostering independent inquiry or intellectual curiosity. In fact, some of Silberman's most telling examples come from reputedly progressive schools where the rhetoric of the administration is belied by the reality of the rulebook. There is a striking and uncomfortable resemblance between Silberman's characterization of the schools and our own description of total institutions in the previous chapter.

Silberman joins many other critics of the school system in attacking their differential treatment of poor and middle-class children, and he brings out one important manifestation of that inequality. He cites a study by anthropologist Eleanor Leacock (1969) in which she interviewed teachers and observed interactions between students and teachers in urban schools serving four types of population: low-income black, low-income white, middle-income black, and middle-income white. She found that teachers of children from middle-income families, both black and white, made stricter demands on children in terms of behavior as well as academic achievement. Leacock also found that teachers' expectations about the likely performance of their students were higher for middle-income children.

A dramatic attempt to demonstrate the impact of teacher expectations on the academic performance of children was carried out by psychologist Robert Rosenthal and his associate Lenore Jacobson in a California elementary school serving lower-income white and Mexican-American students (Rosenthal & Jacobson, 1968). The researchers administered a set of standard intelligence tests to the children, but told the teachers that the tests were new instruments especially designed to detect "sleepers"—children who had given no evidence of special intellectual ability but who could be expected to "bloom" in the future. They then *randomly* picked a group of children who were designated to the teachers as sleepers. At periodic intervals for the next few years they returned to the school and retested all the children on different forms of the same test, and also collected data on classroom performance, grades, and teacher impressions. They found that the children for whom teacher expectations had been artificially raised scored higher in all three categories, at least for the year or two following the original testing! The average IQ difference between the experimental and control groups was about 15.4 points after a year for the first-graders, and 9.5 for the second-graders. (Older children showed no gains.) The Rosenthal & Jacobson study has been severely criticized on methodological grounds (cf. Thorndike, 1969) and so it cannot be said to demonstrate unequivocally the effects of arbitrarily raised expectations. However, together with the Leacock study and many others (see Rosenthal & Jacobson, 1968, Chaps. 1-4 for a review) it gives us strong reason to suspect that teacher expectations play a major role in the kind of socialization that particular children receive in the schools. Of course, teachers are not the only people who have low expectations for the children of the poor. Many studies of attitudes of lower- and middle-class parents have consistently revealed that impoverished parents, perhaps realistically, also set their educational and occupational sights for their children relatively low (see Hess, 1970, especially pp. 474-475, 500-591, for a review). Thus it may be true, as many have argued, that subtle differences in socialization account for the large gaps in cognitive achievement between the children of the poor and those of the middle class. Perhaps part of the reason why schools fail to equip poor children with traditional skills—reading, writing, etc.—is that they reinforce in the children a sense of inferiority, a belief that they cannot learn.

In sum, we have seen that critics of the schools accuse them of unequal treatment of poor and minority children, thus reinforcing the very social divisions that schools are supposed to break down, and of mind-dulling regimentation that erodes the qualities of independence, curiosity, autonomy, and responsibility that schools are supposed to foster. If the critics are even partially right—and we feel that they are—

then the increasing role of the school in socialization is not a development to be hailed with unbridled enthusiasm.

Before leaving this topic, however, we should point out some educational developments that may change the picture in the future. One is the "open classroom," a style of classroom organization that had its start in England and is rapidly being adopted in public and private elementary schools in this country. In open classrooms learning is decentralized. Instead of a teacher drilling or lecturing a roomful of students arranged in neat rows, the teacher breaks the classroom into activity centers equipped with different kinds of books, games, art supplies, and other materials for "individually guided education." Children choose their activities freely. The teacher's job is to supply stimulating materials and ideas, answer questions, and guide the children toward the most instructive uses of their activities. Open classrooms are often "vertically grouped," with children of different ages teaching one another. The aim of the open classroom is to make an institutional reality, not just a stated ideal, out of self-directed learning and instructional methods that meet the individual needs, interests, and learning styles of each child.

Experiences similar in concept to the open classroom have been provided for older children and adolescents in "free schools" (independent schools outside the public system), "alternative schools" (experimental schools within the system), or in special classes and programs within otherwise traditional schools. Typically, free schools offer minimal regulation of the student's day, a wide range of options for study, and academic credit for work done in real-life settings outside the school. An example is Philadelphia's famous Parkway Project, a "school without walls" in which most learning takes place in the city's museums, libraries, industries, and public agencies. Often such experimental programs offer opportunities for personal development outside the intellectual sphere with which schools have traditionally concerned themselves. The Human Relations Seminar described in Chapter 3 is an example of another form of innovative program; in this case, one offered at an elite prep school. The broad goals of such "learning by experience" involve the integration of a child's *thinking* with his *feeling*.

The ideas behind the open classroom and the free school are not new. They have a long history in educational philosophy and were perhaps most completely and cogently expressed by John Dewey.

Moreover, these ideas in their most radical form were given concrete expression in the school established by A. S. Neill. Neill's book *Summerhill: A Radical Approach to Child-Rearing* (1960) was an inspiration for many of the current generation of educational reformers.

Within and outside the public school system there have been many attempts to offset the differential socialization of middle-class children and children of the poor and of minority groups. The most ambitious of these was Project Head Start, a massive, federally funded attempt to provide the children of the poor with a preschool experience that would equip them with cognitive and social skills necessary to function in the school system. Countless other programs, too numerous and varied to describe, have participated in the effort to eradicate the race and class bias of the schools.

Despite claims of spectacular success, and occasional pronouncements of failure, it is still too early to tell whether contemporary educational experiments will in the long run succeed in producing a generation of students who are more independent and less intellectually docile than students in conventional public schools, or whether those experiments will have any noticeable effect at all on the gap between middle-class Americans and the poor. What is clear, however, is that they represent direct efforts at finding alternatives to current patterns of socialization in the schools.

SUMMARY AND CONCLUSION

In this chapter we have examined some potentially significant changes in the way children are reared, both in this society and elsewhere. We began by suggesting that changes in socialization practices can change the character of a society, and we questioned whether planned changes in socialization could be used to build a better society. We have seen that there is reason to believe that unplanned changes have occurred in the socialization of American children, and that some psychologists fear that these changes may have ill effects on our national character. We have also seen that other societies have tried to use changes in child-rearing practices to inculcate values very different from traditional American ideas. Psychologists have been able to discern some of the psychological costs and benefits of these bold experiments. There appears to be truth in the Freudian belief that *any* civilization achieves unity and collective direction only at a price to the individual and his instinctual life. Yet, the success of the Russian educational system and the kibbutz *on their own terms* suggests that a global improvement in society may also be possible *within a given framework of values*. If social scientists in the United States have not taught us how to make our lives better, perhaps part of the reason is our collective inability as citizens to decide what "better" means.

By linking societal change to change in individuals, this chapter completes our circle that began in Chapter 2 with changes produced by the interaction of individuals in the process of psychotherapy. Moreover, the final chapter, like all the others in this book, has confronted us once again with the imperative connections between social science and values. A brief Epilogue highlights these and other general issues raised by our investigation of the role of psychology in understanding and facilitating social change.

Epilogue

You have just finished reading a book on psychology and social change. There is very little doubt that you took the topic to imply "change for the better" and that you have looked in these pages for clues as to how psychology can improve your life, or the lives of people in general. It is worthwhile at this point to step back for a moment to survey the territory we have covered and to identify a few crucial issues that bear on the role of psychology as an agent of social change.

Perhaps you have been frustrated at some points by the apparent incompleteness of current psychological knowledge. Those branches of the field dealing with personality and social behavior are not sciences with the rigor and exactitude of the physical sciences. In all probability they never will achieve that degree of precision; human subjects wriggle and squirm too much under the psychologist's scrutiny to allow his observations and generalizations to stand still either. Perhaps, as social psychologist Kenneth Gergen (1969) has argued, we should view psychology as a species of historical study and learn to relate psychological laws to their social context. The analogy between psychology and physical science may be fundamentally spurious; the inevitable intrusion of moral concerns into psychological investigation, and the fact that the psychologist is himself a specimen of the phenomenon under study, may introduce unavoidable ambiguities into the scientific study of man.

Whether or not these conjectures are accepted (many psychologists do *not* accept them) it is clear that psychology cannot today fill all the hopes and expectations of those who turn to it for direction. Nevertheless the lesson to be drawn is not one of despair, nor of the futility of psychological investigation. We must abandon the expectation that psychology can provide a pat technology for the alteration of human thought, feeling, and action. All that we can ask of a *social* science is that it expand the framework of understanding within which individuals and societies can make humane and ethical choices. With respect to this goal, we feel that the preceding chapters have made evident the past contributions and the future potential of psychology.

In Chapter 2 we saw how psychotherapy can increase the individual's awareness of his own motives and feelings, thus increasing his ability to choose courses of constructive action, relatively free of destructive and self-defeating compulsions. In Chapter 3 we saw how groups can serve similar functions, as well as increasing the individual's ability to accurately perceive others and his sensitivity to the effects of his actions on others. In Chapter 4 we saw how psychological understanding of the structure of institutions can help explain their power to enhance or obstruct changes in the individual. Through such understanding a society potentially can, for better or worse, improve the effectiveness of its institutions for dealing with behavior which that particular society defines as deviant. Finally, in Chapter 5 we saw how an understanding of the socialization process can help a society to design child-care and educational systems to serve its own needs and meet its own values. Thus, psychology has contributed insights and techniques that help individuals and societies to integrate their actions and values.

Perhaps psychology has exerted its most fundamental influence on social change by transforming man's thinking about human nature. Psychological-mindedness is now an integral fiber woven into our culture. For example, the work of Sigmund Freud has become so much a part of out intellectual heritage that we rarely know when we are viewing the world through glasses he provided. Freud's illumination of man's inner life has influenced our literature, drama, and cinema. At a more subliminal level, when we interpret a friend's behavior in terms of unconscious motives, or when we recognize his conflicts or defenses, we are speaking in Freud's language. Thus, psychology has provided new ways of looking at old human problems and, in doing so, has brought about a major social change: it has altered man's consciousness of himself.

Bibliography

Adorno, T. W., Else Frenkel-Brunswick, D. J. Levinson, and R. N. Sanford: *The Authoritarian Personality*, Harper and Row, New York, 1950.

Alschuler, Alfred: "The Origins and Nature of Psychological Education," *Educational Opportunity Forum*, vol. I, no. iv, 1969.

Back, Kurt: *Sensitivity Training and the Search for Salvation*, New York, Russell Sage Foundation, 1972.

Bailyn, L.: "Mass Media and Children: A Study of Exposure Habits and Cognitive Effects," *Psychological Monographs*, 73(1, Whole No. 471), 1959.

Bales, Robert F.: *Personality and Interpersonal Behavior*, Holt, Rinehart and Winston, New York, 1970.

Bandura, A., D. Ross, and S. Ross: "Imitation of Film-Mediated Aggressive Models," *Journal of Abnormal and Social Psychology*, 66:3–11, 1963.

Behavior Today, 3(11):1, March 13, 1972.

Belknap, I.: *Human Problems of a State Mental Hospital*, McGraw-Hill, New York, 1956.

Benedict, Ruth: "Continuities and Discontinuities in Cultural Conditioning," *Psychiatry*, 1:161–167, 1938.
Bennis, Warren G.: "Goals and Meta-Goals of Laboratory Training," *NTL Human Relations Training News*, 6(3):1–4, 1962.
Bennis, Warren G., and Herbert A. Shepard: "A Theory of Group Development," *Human Relations*, 9(4): 1956.
Bettelheim, B.: "Individual and Mass Behavior in Extreme Situations," *Journal of Abnormal and Social Psychology*, 38:417–452, 1943.
Bettelheim, B.: *The Children of the Dream*, Macmillan, New York, 1969.
Bion, W. R.: *Experiences in Groups*, Tavistock Publications, London, 1961.
Bloom, B. L.: *Community Mental Health: A Historical and Critical Analysis*, General Learning Corp. Press, Morristown, N.J., 1973.
Bowerman, C. E., and J. W. Kinch: "Changes in Family and Peer Orientation of Children Between the 4th and 10th Grades," *Social Forces*, 37(3):206–211, 1959.
Braginsky, B. M., D. D. Braginsky, and K. Ring: *Methods of Madness; the Mental Hospital as a Last Resort*, Holt, Rinehart and Winston, New York, 1969.
Bronfenbrenner, U.: "Response to Pressure from Peers Versus Adults Among Soviet and American School Children," *International Journal of Psychology*, 2:199–207, 1967.
Bronfenbrenner, U.: *Two Worlds of Childhood: U.S. and U.S.S.R.*, Russell Sage Foundation, New York, 1970.
Caplan, G.: "Clinical Observations on the Emotional Life of Children in the Communal Settlements in Israel," in M. J. E. Senn (ed.), *Problems of Infancy and Early Childhood: Transactions of the Seventh Conference*, Josiah Macy, Jr. Foundation, 1954.
Caudill, W.: *The Psychiatric Hospital as a Small Society*, Harvard University Press, Cambridge, Mass., 1958.
Clark, K. B., and M. P. Clark: "Emotional Factors in Racial Identification and Preference in Negro Children," *Journal of Negro Education*, 19:341–350, 1950.
Clark, K. B., and M. P. Clark: "Racial Identification and Preferences in Negro Children," in T. M. Newcomb and E. L. Hartley (eds.), *Readings in Social Psychology*, Holt, New York, 1947.
Coleman, J. C.: *Abnormal Psychology and Modern Life*, Scott Foresman, Glenville, Ill., 1964.
Coleman, J. S.: *The Adolescent Society*, Free Press of Glencoe, New York, 1961.

Coleman, J. S., et al.: *Equality of Educational Opportunity*, U.S. Government Printing Office, Washington, D.C., 1966.

Davis, A. J.: "Sexual Assaults in the Philadelphia Prison System," in S. E. Wallace (ed.), *Total Institutions*, Transaction Books, 1971.

Dreeben, R.: *On What Is Learned in School*, Addison-Wesley, Reading, Mass., 1968.

Erikson, Erik H.: *Childhood and Society*, W. W. Norton, New York, 1950.

Erikson, Erik H.: *Gandhi's Truth*, W. W. Norton, New York, 1969.

Eron, L.: "Relationship of TV Viewing Habits and Aggressive Behavior in Children," *Journal of Abnormal and Social Psychology*, 67:193-196, 1963.

Eysenck, H. J.: "Classification and the Problem of Diagnosis," in H. J. Eysenck (ed.), *Handbook of Abnormal Psychology*, Basic Books, New York, 1961.

Feshbach, S.: "Aggression," in P. H. Mussen (ed.), *Carmichael's Manual of Child Psychology*, 3rd ed., John Wiley, New York, 1970.

Feshbach, S., and R. D. Singer: *Television and Aggression*, Jossey-Bass, San Francisco, 1971.

Freeman, H. E., and J. M. Giovannoni: "Social Psychology of Mental Health," in G. Lindzey and E. Aronson (eds.), *The Handbook of Social Psychology*, Addison-Wesley, Reading, Mass., 1969, pp. 660-719.

Freud, S.: *Civilization and Its Discontents* (translated by James Strachey), W. W. Norton, New York, 1962. Originally published under the title *Das Unbehangen in der Kultur*, Internationaler Psychoanalytischer Verlag, Vienna, 1930.

Freud, S.: "Civilized Sexual Morality and Modern Nervous Illness," in *The Standard Edition of the Complete Psychological Works of Sigmund Freud*, Hogarth Press, London, 1953, vol. 9.

Freud, S.: *Group Psychology and the Analysis of the Ego*, Liveright, New York, 1951.

Geller, W.: "The Problem of Prisons—A Way Out?", *The Humanist*, 32(3):24-33, May-June 1972.

Gendlin, Eugene T.: "A Theory of Personality Change," in Philip Worchel and Donn Byrne (eds.), *Personality Change*, John Wiley, New York, 1964.

Gendlin, Eugene T.: *Experiencing and the Creation of Meaning*, Free Press, Glencoe, Ill., 1962.

Gendlin, Eugene T., et al.: "Focusing Ability in Psychotherapy, Personality, and Creativity," in J. Shlien (ed.), *Research in Psychotherapy*,

Volume III, American Psychological Association, Washington, D.C., 1967.

Gergen, K. J.: *The Psychology of Behavior Exchange,* Addison-Wesley, Reading, Mass., 1969.

Gibb, Jack R., and M. Lorranine: "Role Freedom in a TORI Group," in Arthur Burton (ed.), *Encounter,* Jossey-Bass, San Francisco, 1970.

Glaser, D.: *The Effectiveness of a Prison and Parole System,* Bobbs-Merrill, Indianapolis, Ind., 1964.

Goffman, E.: *Asylums,* Doubleday, Garden City, New York, 1961.

Goldenberg, I. Ira: *Build Me a Mountain,* The MIT Press, Cambridge, Mass., 1971.

Greenberg, D. F.: "Rehabilitation Is Still Punishment," *The Humanist,* 32(3):28–29, May–June 1972.

Greenblatt, M., R. H. York, and E. L. Brown: *From Custodial to Therapeutic Care in Mental Hospitals,* Russell Sage Foundation, New York, 1955.

Greenson, Ralph: *The Technique and Practice of Psychoanalysis,* International Universities Press, New York, 1967, vol. I.

Hartup, W. W.: "Peer Interaction and Social Organization," in P. H. Mussen (ed.), *Carmichael's Manual of Child Psychology,* 3rd ed., John Wiley, New York, 1970.

Hess, R. D.: "Social Class and Ethnic Influences on Socialization," in P. H. Mussen (ed.), *Carmichael's Manual of Child Psychology,* 3rd ed., John Wiley, New York, 1970.

Himmelweit, H. T., A. N. Oppenheim, and P. Vince: *Television and the Child,* Oxford University Press, New York, 1958.

Hollingshead, August B., and Frederick C. Redlich: *Social Class and Mental Illness,* John Wiley, New York, 1958.

Jackson, B.: "A Day in the Life of the Arkansas Penitentiary," *Transaction: Social Science and Modern Society,* 9(6, Whole No. 76), 30–35, April 1972.

Jencks, C.: "A Reappraisal of the Most Controversial Educational Document of our Time," *New York Times,* August 10, 1969.

Jencks, C. S., et al.: *Inequality: A Reassessment of the Effects of Family and Schooling in America,* Basic Books, New York, 1972.

Joint Commission on Mental Illness and Health, *Action for Mental Health,* Basic Books, 1961.

Jones, Ernest: *The Life and Work of Sigmund Freud,* Doubleday Anchor Books, New York, 1963.

Jones, M.: *The Therapeutic Community*, Basic Books, New York, 1953.
Kelman, H. C.: "Processes of Opinion Change," *Public Opinion Quarterly*, 25:57–78, 1961.
Keniston, K.: *Young Radicals; Notes on Committed Youth*, Harcourt, Brace and World, New York, 1968.
Kesey, K.: *One Flew Over the Cuckoo's Nest*, Viking Press, New York, 1962.
Kluckhohn, Clyde: "Values and Value Orientations in the Theory of Action," in Talcott Parsons and Edward A. Shils (eds.), *Toward a General Theory of Action*, Harvard University Press, Cambridge, Mass., 1951.
Kluckhohn, Clyde, Henry A. Murray, and David M. Schneider (eds.), *Personality in Nature, Society, and Culture*, Alfred A. Knopf, New York, 1967.
Kluckhohn, Florence: "Dominant and Variant Value Orientations," in Clyde Kluckhohn, Henry A. Murray, and David M. Schneider (eds.), *Personality in Nature, Society, and Culture*, Alfred A. Knopf, New York, 1967.
Laing, R. D.: *Self and Others*, Pantheon Books, New York, 1961.
Laing, R. D.: *The Divided Self*, Penguin Books, Baltimore, 1965.
Laing, R. D.: "The Obvious," in Hendrik M. Ruitenbeek (ed.), *Going Crazy*, Bantam Books, New York, 1972.
Leacock, E. B.: *Teaching and Learning in City Schools*, Basic Books, New York, 1969.
Lesser, G. S.: "Learning, Teaching and Television Production for Children: The Experience of *Sesame Street*," *Harvard Educational Review*, 42:232–272, 1972.
Lieberman, Morton A., Irvin D. Yalom, and Matthew B. Miles: *Encounter Groups: First Facts*, Basic Books, New York, 1973.
Liebert, R. M., M. D. Sobol, and E. S. Davidson: "Catharsis of Aggression Among Institutionalized Boys: Fact or Artifact?", in G. A. Comstock, E. A. Rubenstein, and J. P. Murray (eds.), *Television and Social Behavior*, vol. 5, *Television's Effects: Further Explorations*, U.S. Government Printing Office, Washington, D.C., 1971. (A reply by S. Feshbach and R. D. Singer, and further discussion, appears in the same volume.)
Lifton, R. J.: *Thought Reform and the Psychology of Totalism: A Study of Brainwashing in China*, W. W. Norton, New York, 1961.
Luft, Joseph: *Group Processes: An Introduction to Group Dynamics*, National Press, Palo Alto, Calif., 1963.

Lyle, J., and H. Hoffman: "Children's Use of Television and Other Media," in E. A. Rubenstein, G. A. Comstock, and J. P. Murray (eds.), *Television and Social Behavior*, vol. 5, *Television in Day-To-Day Life: Patterns of Use*, U.S. Government Printing Office, Washington, D.C., 1971.

Maher, Brendan: *Principles of Psychopathology*, McGraw-Hill, New York, 1966.

Mann, Richard: *Interpersonal Styles and Group Development*, John Wiley, New York, 1967.

Marcuse, H.: *Eros and Civilization*, Beacon Press, Boston, 1955.

Massar, Barbara: *A Study of Experiencing Learning in Adolescent Self-Analytic Groups*, unpublished doctoral dissertation, Harvard Graduate School of Education, 1972.

McClelland, David C., and David G. Winter: *Motivating Economic Achievement*, The Free Press, New York, 1969.

McGregor, Douglas M.: "The Human Side of Enterprise," in Warren G. Bennis, Kenneth D. Benne, and Robert Chin (eds.), *The Planning of Change*, Holt, Rinehart and Winston, New York, 1961.

Mills, Theodore M.: *Group Transformation*, Prentice-Hall, Englewood Cliffs, N.J., 1964.

Moreno, J. L.: *Who Shall Survive?*, Beacon House, New York, 1953.

Mosher, R., and N. Sprinthall: "Psychological Education: A Means to Promote Personal Development During Adolescence," *The Counseling Psychologist*, vol. 2, no. 4, 1971.

Mosteller, F., and D. P. Moynihan (eds.): *On Equality of Educational Opportunity*, Vintage Books, New York, 1972.

National Clearing House for Mental Health Information, Statistical Note #33, National Institute of Mental Health, Biometry Branch, Survey and Report Section, 1971.

Neill, A. S.: *Summerhill: A Radical Approach to Child-Rearing*, Hart, New York, 1960.

Parsons, Talcott: "Social Structure and the Development of Personality: Freud's Contribution to the Integration of Psychology and Sociology," in Neil J. Smelser (ed.), *Personality and Social Systems*, John Wiley, New York, 1963.

Parsons, Talcott, and Edward A. Shils (eds.): *Toward a General Theory of Action*, Harvard University Press, Cambridge, Mass., 1951.

Piaget, Jean: *Six Psychological Studies*, Vintage Books, New York, 1968.

Pizer, Stuart A.: *Group Interaction and Ego-Integration in Adolescence*, unpublished doctoral dissertation, Harvard University, Cambridge, Mass., 1972.

Polster, Erving: "Encounter in Community," in Arthur Burton (ed.), *Encounter*, Jossey-Bass, San Francisco, 1970.
Rapoport, R. N.: *Community As Doctor*, Tavistock Publications, London, 1960.
Rodgers, R. R., U. Bronfenbrenner, and E. C. Devereux: "Standards of Social Behavior Among Children in Four Cultures," *International Journal of Psychology*, 3:31–41, 1968.
Rogers, Carl: *On Encounter Groups*, Harper and Row, New York, 1970.
Rogers, Carl: "The Process of the Basic Encounter Group," in James Bugental (ed.), *Challenges of Humanistic Psychology*, McGraw-Hill, New York, 1967.
Rogers, Carl (ed.): *The Therapeutic Relationship and Its Impact*, The University of Wisconsin Press, Madison, 1967.
Rosenhan, D. L.: "On Being Sane in Insane Places," *Science*, **179**(4070):250–258, 1973.
Rosenhan, D. L. "The Natural Socialization of Altruistic Autonomy," in J. Macaulay and L. Berkowitz (eds.), *Altruism and Helping Behavior*, Academic Press, New York, 1970.
Rosenthal, R., and L. Jacobson: *Pygmalion in the Classroom*, Holt, Rinehart and Winston, 1968.
Rothman, D. J.: *The Discovery of the Asylum: Social Order and Disorder in the New Republic*, Little, Brown, Boston, 1971.
Schein, E. H.: "The Chinese Indoctrination Program for Prisoners of War: A Study of Attempted 'Brainwashing,'" *Psychiatry*, 19:149–172, 1956.
Sears, R. R., E. Maccoby, and H. Levin: *Patterns of Child-Rearing*, Row, Peterson, Evanston, Ill., 1957.
Shiloh, A.: "Sanctuary or Prison—Responses to Life in a Mental Hospital," in S. E. Wallace (ed.), *Total Institutions*, Transaction Books, 1971.
Silberman, C. E.: *Crisis in the Classroom*, Random House, New York, 1970.
Skinner, B. F.: *Beyond Freedom and Dignity*, Knopf, New York, 1971.
Skinner, B. F.: *Walden Two*, Macmillan, New York, 1948.
Slater, Philip: *Microcosm*, John Wiley, New York, 1966.
Slater, Philip: *The Pursuit of Loneliness*, Beacon Press, Boston, 1970.
Spiro, M. E.: *Children of the Kibbutz*, Harvard University Press, Cambridge, Mass., 1958.
Spiro, M. E.: *Kibbutz: Venture in Utopia*, Harvard University Press, Cambridge, Mass., 1956.

Stanton, A. H., and M. S. Schwartz: *The Mental Hospital,* Basic Books, New York, 1954.

Statistical Abstracts of the U.S., U.S. Department of Commerce; U.S. Government Printing Office, Washington, D.C., 1971.

Sullivan, Harry Stack: *The Interpersonal Theory of Psychiatry,* W. W. Norton, New York, 1953.

Surgeon General's Scientific Advisory Committee on Television and Social Behavior, *Television and Growing Up: The Impact of Televised Violence,* U.S. Government Printing Office, Washington, D.C., 1972.

Sykes, J. G.: *The Society of Captives,* Princeton University Press, N.J., 1958.

Szasz, Thomas: *Ideology and Insanity,* Doubleday Anchor Books, New York, 1970.

Talbot, E., S. C. Miller, and R. B. White: "Some Antitherapeutic Side Effects of Hospitalization and Psychotherapy," *Psychiatry,* 27:170–176, 1964.

Thomas, P.: *Down These Mean Streets,* Knopf, New York, 1967.

Thorndike, R. L.: Review of R. Rosenthal and L. Jacobson, *Pygmalion in the Classroom, Teachers' College Record,* 70(8):805–807, 1969.

Ullman, L. P., and L. Krasner (eds.): *Case Studies in Behavior Modification,* Holt, Rinehart and Winston, New York, 1965.

U.S. Public Health Service: "Patients in State and County Mental Hospitals 1967," U.S. Government Printing Office, Publication No. 1921, Washington, D.C., 1969.

Ward, L. S.: "Effects of Television Advertising on Children and Adolescents," in E. A. Rubenstein, G. A. Comstock, and J. P. Murray (eds.), *Television and Social Behavior,* vol. 4, *Television in Day-To-Day Life: Patterns of Use,* U.S. Government Printing Office, Washington, D.C., 1971.

Whitaker, Dorothy S., and Morton Lieberman: *Psychotherapy Through the Group Process,* Atherton Press, New York, 1964.

White, Robert W.: *The Abnormal Personality,* Ronald, New York, 1964.

Whiting, John M., and Irvin L. Child: *Child Training and Personality,* Yale University Press, New Haven, 1953.

Wilson, J. Q.: "If Every Criminal Knew He Would Be Punished If Caught . . .", *New York Times Magazine,* Sunday, Jan. 28, 1973, pp. 9ff.

Wolpe, Joseph: *Psychotherapy by Reciprocal Inhibition,* Stanford University Press, Stanford, Calif., 1958.

Yalom, Irvin D.: *The Theory and Practice of Group Psychotherapy,* Basic Books, New York, 1970.

Zimbardo, P. G.: "Pathology of Imprisonment," *Transaction: Social Science and Modern Society,* 9(Whole No. 76), 4–8, April 1972.

Index

Acceptance:
  in inmate culture, 91
  self-, in encounter groups, 48
Accurate empathic understanding, 15-16, 21, 25
Achievement as value, 149, 150
Achievement motive, 28
Activism, political, 7
Adaptation (adjustment), 4, 20, 27
  of inmates to total institutions, 95
  of mental patients, 115, 117
  (*See also* Conformity)
Adoption, group, 135
Affect, flattening of, 132
Affection in T-groups, 44
Aggression (aggressiveness):
  in groups, 43, 46
  in Israeli kibbutzim, 131
  of Soviet children, 136
  television violence and, 142-145
Aggressive drives, Freud's view of, 126
Alienative tendency in inmate culture, 92
Animals, punishment in training of, 88

Anxieties:
  in aversive conditioning, 24, 25
  childhood, 29-31
  desensitization techniques and, 23
  in T-groups, 44, 46
  universal, 30
Application, global, 19-21
Approval in inmate culture, 91
Assertive behavior, training in, 25
Asylums (*see* Mental hospitals)
Authoritarian personality, 28
Authority:
  inmates' patterns of, 90, 92
  of staff in total institutions, 89
  in T-groups, 42-44, 49
Autonomy, personal, 5, 21, 30
  in groups, 36
Aversive conditioning, 24

Barometric events in T-groups, 45
Basic assumptions, Bion's model of, 42, 43
Behavior:
  antisocial: American children, 136, 137

Behavior:
    Israel kibbutzim, 131
    Soviet Union, 136, 137
    (*See also* Crime)
  assertive, training in, 25
  encounter groups and changes in, 49
Behavior control:
  as a function of society, 123–124
  inmate culture and, 90, 91
  in total institutions, 87–89
Behavior modification:
  child development and, 127, 128
  (*See also* Behavior therapy)
Behavior therapy:
  criticism of, 25
  in mental hospitals, 118
  techniques of, 23–25
Behavioral psychology, regulatory systems of total institutions and, 86, 87
Belonging in groups, 36
Black children, school system and, 2, 3, 148, 151
Blacks, 2
  in prison, 96, 106
Boredom in psychotherapy, 13–14

Caring for client, therapist's, 14–15
Catharsis:
  in T-groups, 45
  television violence and, 142, 145
Child development (child rearing; socialization), 6–7, 123–158

Child development:
  crosscultural perspective on, 125–129
  Erikson's view of, 28–31, 125, 127
  family's role, 133, 138–140
  Freud's view of, 126–127
  in Israeli kibbutzim, 129–132
  peer group's role, 135, 139–141
  school's role, 147–156
  Skinner's view of, 127–128
  in Soviet Union, 132–138
  television's role, 141–146
  in United States, 133–155
  (*See also* Education)
Childhood, psychohistory and, 28–31
Civilization, Freud's view of, 126–127, 154–155
Class, social:
  education and, 148, 151, 152, 154
  mental illness and, 22
Client-centered therapy, 9, 39
Closeness:
  in encounter groups, 49
  (*See also* Intimacy)
Codes, inmate, 92–94
Cognitive skills, United States school system and, 147–148
Cohesiveness:
  as function of society, 123
  of inmate cultures, 92
  (*See also* Solidarity)
Collectivism, Soviet emphasis on, 135
Colonization:
  of mental patients, 115–116

Colonization:
  of prison inmates, 94, 95
Communes, 124
  (*See also* Israeli kibbutzim)
Communist morality, 134, 135
Community development, T-groups and, 77
Community mental health centers, 119-120
Compliance, behavior control and, 89
Conceptual monotony, 15
Conceptualization:
  experiencing process and, 16, 17
  psychotherapeutic process and, 16, 17
  (*See also* Thinking)
Conditioning:
  aversive, 24
  operant, 24, 118
Confinement in total institutions, 86
Conflict resolution, T-group techniques for, 77-78
Conformity:
  American school system and, 151
  of Soviet children, 133
  (*See also* Adaptation)
Confrontation in encounter groups, 48
Congruence, 13-14
Consciousness raising, 27
Consciousness-raising groups, Women's Liberation, 35
Consensual validation as subphase of group life, 46-47
Conservatives, media and, 2

Control:
  behavior: as function of society, 123-124
  inmate culture, 90, 91
  total institutions, 87-89
  total institutions' systems of, 84-90
Conversion of inmates, 94-95
Counterculture, inmate, 90-93
Counterdependence-fight as subphase of group life, 44
Counterdependence in groups, 43-45
Counterpersonal individuals, 43, 46
Courts, prison system and, 97
Crimes:
  economic, 97, 103, 107
  high-recidivism, 103-104, 107
  low-recidivism, 103
  nineteenth century view of, 82-83, 121
  social character of, 121-122
  violent, 97, 103
Criminals, 81
  career, 103-104
  community treatment programs for, 102
  nineteenth century treatment of, 82-83
  (*See also* Prison inmates)
Crises, developmental, 125
Culture:
  child development and, 125-129
  Erikson's view of, 27-30, 125, 127
  Freud's view of, 126-127
  inmate, 90-94
  psychohistory and, 27-30

Culture and personality school, 27-28, 125

Defenses (defensive mechanisms; defensive modalities):
  in groups, 42, 43, 48, 50
  of prison inmates, 105-106
Dependence-flight as subphase of group life, 44
Dependence phase of T-groups, 44-45
Dependency in groups, 42, 43
Desensitization techniques, 23-24
Deterrence as goal of prisons, 97-99
  effectiveness of, 101, 102, 105
Development, child (*see* Child Development)
Developmental crises, 125
Developmental psychology, 124
Direct reference, 16-21
  global application of, 19-20
  referent movement and, 20
  unfolding of, 18-19
Discipline:
  of American children, 133, 136
  of Soviet children, 133-136
Discussion, group, 31, 32
Disenchantment-fight as subphase of group life, 46
Drug addicts, 103
Drug users, 91
Drugs, mental hospitals' use of, 87, 119

Eclectic psychotherapy, 9, 21
Ecology, 7-8
Economic crimes, 97, 103, 107
Economic deprivation of prison inmates, 100
Education (school system), 129
  in Israeli kibbutzim, 130, 155
  psychological, T-groups' implications for, 75-77
  in Soviet Union, 124, 133-137, 155
  in United States, 147-154
    experimental schools, 153-154
    social class, 148, 151, 152, 154
    teachers' expectations, 151-152
    values and norms, 148-150
Ego relatedness, T-group experience and, 76
Egocentricity, adolescent, 72
Empathic understanding, accurate, 15-16, 21, 25
Enchantment-flight as subphase of group life, 46
Encounter groups, 35, 39, 47-50
  conflict resolution and, 78
  goals of, 49-50
  intergroup relations and, 77
  T-groups compared to, 48-50
Ethic, Soviet, 135
Exchange systems, inmate, 90-91
Existential analysis, 9
Expectations:
  of staff toward inmates of total institutions, 85-86
  of teachers toward children, 151-152
Experience, shared, 36

Experiencing:
  process of, 16-17
  T-groups and increase in measure of, 76

Families, 12, 27
  socialization and, 124
    American families, 133, 138-140
    Soviet families, 133, 134
Fears, infantile, 29
Feedback in groups, 36, 38, 41, 42, 48
Feeling process, 16
Feelings:
  expression of: in encounter groups, 47-49
    Israeli kibbutzim, 132
  (*See also* Self-expression)
  (*See also* Direct reference)
Feminists, 124
  (*See also* Women's Liberation movement)
Focusing, 17-20
Freedom:
  in encounter groups, 48
  responsibility and, 5
  Skinner's view of, 128

Gay Lib movement, 27
Generation gap, 2
Global application, 19-21
Group adoption in Soviet Union, 135
Group discussion, 31, 32
Group therapy, 39-40, 108
Groups:
  peer: socialization and, 124

Groups:
    American children, 135, 139-141
    Israeli kibbutzim, 132
    Soviet Union, 135, 137
  psychological, 6, 34-40, 157
    applications and implications, 75-79
    criticized as instruments of social change, 52-53
    encounter (*see* Encounter groups)
    general model of, 35-37
    history, 37-40
    illustrative case study, 53-75
    literature, 34
    research, 50-52
    T-groups (*see* T-groups)
  youth, Soviet state-run, 135-136
Guilt of prison inmates, 105

Half-way houses for ex-convicts, 107
Helping relationships in encounter groups, 48, 49
Hidden agendas (unfinished business) in groups, 42, 43, 46
Homosexuals (homosexuality):
  aversive conditioning of, 24-25
  in prisons, 91-93, 99-101
Hostility:
  in groups, 43, 44
  (*See also* Aggression)
Humanization, group techniques and, 78-79

I-Thou encounter, 49
Identification of inmates, 89
Incapacitation as goal of prisons, 97, 99
Independence as value, 149, 150
Independent individuals in groups, 43
Indians, American, 125-126
Individualism, 42, 46
Industry, group techniques used by, 78
Inhibition, reciprocal, 23
Inmates of total institutions:
  psychological world of, 90-95
  (*See also* Mental patients; Prison inmates)
Insecurity, physical, 100-101
Insight:
  psychoanalytic, 28
  psychotherapeutic, 19, 21
  self- (self-awareness; self-knowledge), 41, 50, 76
Institutions, 6, 80-122, 157
  total (*see* Total institutions)
  (*See also* Mental hospitals; Prisons)
Integration:
  personal, 5
    adolescents, 76
    groups, 37
  racial (desegregation), 2, 3
Interdependence:
  in groups, 36
  as phase of T-groups, 44, 46-47
Intergroup relations, T-groups and, 77

Internalization:
  in groups, 37
  of inmates in total institutions, 89, 95
Intimacy:
  in groups, 43, 44, 46, 49, 50
  in Israeli kibbutzim, 132
  (*See also* Closeness)
Intransigence of inmates, 93-95
Israeli kibbutzim, 124, 128-132

Jails (*see* Prisons)
Jews, 26
Jo-Hari Window, 40-42

Kevutza, 130
Kibbutzim, Israeli, 124, 128-132
Kindergartens, Israeli, 130

Laboratory training groups (*see* T-groups)
Leaders, group, 35, 38
  encounter groups, 47
  T-groups, 42-45
  typology of styles of, 51-52
Learning theory, 23
Life review as stage of group life, 47

Madness, radical therapists' view of, 26
Manipulation, 25, 30, 31, 42
Meaning, experiencing process and, 16-17
Media:
  social changes as seen by, 1-2
  (*See also* Television)

INDEX

Mental health centers, community, 119-120
Mental hospitals (asylums), 6, 108-121
  effectiveness of, 112-117
  goals of, 111-112
  patients of (*see* Mental patients)
  population of, 111, 119
  reform and changes in, 117-121
  staff of, 84, 114
    control and regulatory systems, 86-90
    expectations regarding patients, 85-86
    impression management by patients, 116-117
    Rosenhan's study of, 109-110
  as therapeutic community, 118
  as total institution (*see* Total institutions)
Mental illness, 81
  medical model of, 111, 112
  myth of, 25
  nineteenth century view of, 82-83, 121
  social character of, 121-122
  social class and, 22
  (*See also* Madness; Schizophrenics)
Mental patients:
  colonized vs. institutionalized, 115-116
  culture of, 91-93
Mental patients:
  impression management by, 116-117
  legal and civil rights of, 120-121
  pseudo-, Rosenhan's study of, 109-110
  release rates for, 112-113, 118-119
  staff of mental hospitals and:
    control and regulatory systems, 86-90
    expectations regarding patients, 85-86
"Messing-up" phenomenon, 94
Metapelets, 130
Mexican-American children, educational system and, 148, 151-152
Milling-around period in encounter groups, 47
Misbehavior (antisocial behavior):
  of American children, 136, 137
  in Israeli kibbutzim, 131
  in Soviet Union, 136, 137
Morality, Soviet, 135
Motivation-training programs, 77
Murder, 103

National character, 28
Nurseries in Israeli kibbutzim, 130

Obedience of Soviet children, 133, 136
Open classroom schools, 153-154

Operant conditioning, 24, 118
Order:
  socialization and, 123
    American schools, 151
    Soviet Union, 136
  (*See also* Control)
Overpersonal individuals in T-groups, 43, 46

Pairing in groups, 42, 43
Panics, collective, 30
Paranoid projection, 27
Paroling of prison inmates, 88, 99, 101, 106
Peer groups, socialization and, 124
  American children and, 135, 139-141
  Israeli kibbutzim and, 132
  in Soviet Union, 135, 137
Penal system (*see* Prisons)
Personality change, psychotherapy and process of, 16-20
Personality theory, Erikson's, 28
Personality types in groups, 43
  of leaders, 51-52
Phobia, desensitization techniques in treatment of, 23-24
Physical insecurity of prison inmates, 100-101
Plea bargaining, 97
Political activism, 7
Poor, the, mental health centers and, 120
Population growth, 7

Poverty, economic crimes and, 103, 107
Power in T-groups, 44, 49
Prison inmates:
  culture of, 90-93
  defense mechanisms of, 105-106
  economic deprivation of, 100
  furloughs for, 106
  homosexuality of, 91-93, 99-101
  incapacitation of, 97, 99
  indeterminate sentencing of, 107-108
  individual responses of, 93-95
  organizations of former, 107
  paroling of, 88, 99, 101, 106
  physical insecurity of, 100-101
  punishment of, 86-87
  recidivism rate for, 101-103, 107
  reform (rehabilitation) of:
    assessment of effectiveness of, 101, 102
    failure, 104, 105
    as goal of prison system, 97-99
  retribution of society against, 97-100
  sexual deprivation of, 100-101
  staff of prisons and: control and regulatory systems, 86-90, 98-99
    expectations regarding prisoners, 85-86
    inmate culture, 90-92
    prison reform, 106

Prisons, 6, 96–108
  actual changes produced by, 99–106
  degrading effect of, study on, 104–105
  federal and state, 96, 97
  goals of, 97–99
  inmates of (*see* Prison inmates)
  population of, 96, 106
  reform of, 106–108
  staff of (*see* Prison inmates, staff of prisons and)
  as total institutions (*see* Total institutions)
  town and municipal, 96–97
Privileges in total institutions, 86–88
Probation of prison inmates, 106
Progress, 28
Projection, 29
  paranoid, 27
Propaganda, political, 27
Psychiatric social workers, 119
Psychoanalysis, 9–11
  child development and, 125
  group therapy and, 40
  psychohistory and, 28
  recovery rate in, 21
  resistance in, 16
  training, 14
Psychobiography, 27
Psychodrama, 39, 77
Psychohistory, 27–32
Psychologists:
  responsibility of, 4
  social change and role of, 3–8
Psychology, developmental, 124
Psychosis, 113

Psychotherapists:
  accurate empathic understanding of, 15–16
  congruence of, 13–14
  social class origins of, 22–23
  training of, 14
  unconditional positive regard of, 14–15
Psychotherapy, 157
  alternatives to traditional (*see* Behavior therapy; Radical therapy)
  client-centered, 9, 39
  critics of traditional, 20–23
  cure-research aspects of, 9, 11
  eclectic, 9, 21
  effectiveness (success) of: conditions, 12–16
    criteria, 21–22
    criticisms, 21, 22
  existential, 9
  Freud's influence on, 10–11
  gestalt, 9
  group, 39–40, 108
  influential individuals and, 10–11
  major schools of, 9–10
  nature of, 12
  personal relationship of therapist and client in, 13–16
  process of, 12
    personality changes, 16–20
  success rate of, 12–13, 21
  transactional, 9
Punishment:
  in aversive conditioning, 24, 25
  in total institutions, 86–90
    inmate culture, 91

Race relations, 7
Radical therapy, 25-27
Radicals:
  media and, 2
  young (student), 8, 141
Rape, homosexual, 100-101
Rational analysis stage in groups, 45, 47
Recidivism rate of prison inmates, 101-103, 107
Reciprocal inhibition, 23
Reference (referent), direct, 16-21
  global application of, 19-20
  referent movement and, 20, 21
  unfolding of, 18-19
Referent movement, 20, 21
Reform of prison inmates (rehabilitation):
  assessment of effectiveness of, 101, 102
  failure of, 104, 105
  as goal of prison system, 97-99
Regimentation:
  in prisons, 98-99
  of Soviet children, 134-135
Rehabilitation (*see* Reform of prison inmates)
Reinforcers (reinforcements):
  aversive, 86
  in operant conditioning, 24
  in total institutions, 86-89
  inmate culture, 90, 91
Relaxation in behavior therapy, 23-24
Resistance in psychoanalysis, 16
Resolution-catharsis as subphase of group life, 45

Responsibility:
  of individuals, 4-5
  mental patients' relief from, 117
  of psychologists, 4
Restraints, physical, 86, 87
Retribution as goal of prisons, 97-100
"Return of the repressed, the," 20
Rewards (*see* Reinforcers)
Role models:
  sex, 124, 131
  socialization and, 125, 131
  American children, 139
Role playing in groups, 36, 37
Russia, child development in, 132-138

Sabras, 131, 132
Schizophrenics, 113
Schools, 124
  community control of, 3
  free or alternative, 153-154
  segregation in, 2, 3
  (*See also* Education)
Self-acceptance in encounter groups, 48
Self-awareness (self-insight; self-knowledge, 5
  groups and, 41, 50, 76
Self-disclosure (self-expression; self-revelation) in groups, 41, 42, 47, 48
Self-exploration, 15, 16
Self-reliance, 42
Sensitivity training groups (*see* T-groups)

INDEX

Sex roles, 124, 131
Sexual deprivation of prison
 inmates, 100
Sexual drives, Freud's view of,
 126–127
Sexual revolution, 2
Shared experience in groups, 36
Shock therapy, 87, 108
Sioux Indians, 28, 125, 126
Situational withdrawal of
 inmates, 94, 95
Social class:
 education and, 148, 151, 152,
  154
 mental illness and, 22
Social system, 6
Social workers, psychiatric, 119
Socialization (*see* Child development)
Solidarity:
 of inmate culture, 92
 of T-groups, 45, 46
Soviet Union, child development
 in, 132–138
Specificity as value, 149–150
Subculture, inmate, 90–94
Subgroups in T-groups, 44–46

T-groups, 37–79
 applications and implications
  of, 75–79
 case study of, 53–75
 critics of, 52–53
 dependence phase of, 44–45
 educational implications of,
  75–77
 encounter groups compared
  to, 48–50
 feedback in, 38, 41, 42, 48

T-groups:
 goals of, 42–43, 49
 Jo-Hari Window diagram of,
  40–42
 interdependence phase of, **44**,
  46–47
 leaders of, 42–45
 obstacles to interpersonal
  communication in, 42, 43,
  49
 personality types in, 43
Television, socialization and,
 124, 141–146
Tension, 21
 unfolding of direct referent
  and, 18–19
Therapeutic community, mental
 hospitals as, 118
Therapists (*see* Psychotherapists)
Therapy:
 behavior: criticism of, 25
  mental hospitals, 118
  techniques, 23–25
 group, 39–40, 108
 radical, 25–27
 shock, 87, 108
 (*See also* Psychotherapy)
Thinking:
 and psychological education in
  T-groups, 75–77
 (*See also* Conceptualization)
Thought reform program, 92
Token economies, 24, 118
Tolerance of deviant behavior
 in mental hospitals, 114–115
Total institutions, 83–96, 151
 as agents of change, 95–96
 definition of, 83–84

Total institutions:
  degrading effects of, 104
  future of, 121–122
  individual responses of inmates in, 93–95
  inmate culture in, 90–94
  staff of, 84–90
  and pressure for control, 84–86
  and means and limits of control, 86–90
Totalitarianism, 4
  of prisons, 107
Training:
  in assertive behavior, 25
  motivation, 77
  of psychotherapists, 14
  vocational, in prisons, 107
Training groups (*see* T-groups)
Transference emotionality, 45
Transparency of therapist, 13
Trust in groups, 35, 47, 48

Understanding:
  accurate empathic, 15–16, 21, 25
  (*See also* Congruence)
Unfinished business (hidden agendas) in groups, 42, 43, 46
United States, child development in, 133–155

United States:
  family's role in, 133, 138–140
  peer group's role in, 135, 139–141
  school's role in, 147–154
  television's role in, 141–146
Universalism as value, 149, 150
Urbanization, 7
Utopias, 123, 127

Valence tendencies of individuals, 43
Values, socialization and, 123–125, 155
  American children and, 140, 141, 148–150
  Soviet children and, 135, 137
Veterans, World War II, 39, 40
Vietnam war, 8, 26–27
Violence, television, 142–146
Vocational training in prisons, 107

Withdrawal, situational, 94, 95
Women, 2
Women's Liberation movement, 27, 35
  (*See also* Feminists)
Workers, group techniques and, 78

Youth groups, Soviet, 135–136